Making
Nonprofits Work

CENTER
for PUBLIC
SERVICE

The Brookings Institution established the Center for Public Service in 1999 to improve the odds that America's most talented citizens will choose careers in the public service. Toward that goal, the center is committed to rigorous research and practical recommendations for making public service more attractive, be it in traditional government settings, nonprofit agencies, or the growing number of private firms that provide services once delivered inside government. As the center's logo suggests, the single-sectored, government-centered public service of the 1970s has been replaced by the multisectored, highly mobile public service of today. The center was created to track the rise of this new public service, while making sure that both government and the nonprofit sector can compete for their fair share of talent in an ever-tightening labor market.

As part of this effort, the Center for Public Service is committed to publishing timely reports on the state of the public service. These reports, which vary in length from short reports to books, attempt to lay the foundation for long needed policy reforms. Because these reports are designed to move quickly into publication, some will not be verified to the same level of detail as other Brookings publications. As with all Brookings publications, the judgments, conclusions, and recommendations presented in any individual study are solely those of the author or authors and should not be attributed to the trustees, officers, or other staff members of the institution.

THE ASPEN⟩INSTITUTE

The Nonprofit Sector Research Fund awards research grants and organizes convenings to expand knowledge of the nonprofit sector and philanthropy, improve nonprofit practices, and inform public policy related to nonprofits. Established at The Aspen Institute in 1991, the Fund seeks to enhance both the quantity and quality of nonprofit research by increasing the legitimacy and visibility of nonprofit scholarship; encouraging new investment in sector research; supporting the exploration of tough, neglected questions; and enlarging the number of creative scholars and practitioners interested in pursuing nonprofit studies.

The Nonprofit Sector Research Fund's programs are supported by the Carnegie Corporation of New York, The Ford Foundation, William Randolph Hearst Foundation, The James Irvine Foundation, W. K. Kellogg Foundation, Charles Stewart Mott Foundation, The David and Lucile Packard Foundation, and others.

PAUL C. LIGHT

Making Nonprofits Work

A REPORT ON THE TIDES OF NONPROFIT MANAGEMENT REFORM

THE ASPEN INSTITUTE
BROOKINGS INSTITUTION PRESS
Washington, D.C.

Copyright © 2000
THE BROOKINGS INSTITUTION
1775 Massachusetts Avenue, N.W., Washington, D.C. 20036
www.brookings.edu

Library of Congress Cataloging-in-Publication data

Light, Paul C.
Making nonprofits work: a report on the tides of nonprofit management reform / Paul C. Light.
    p.   cm.
Includes bibliographical references and index.
ISBN 0-8157-5245-8 (pb : acid-free)
    1. Nonprofit organizations—Management.   2. Organizational effectiveness.   3. Management.   I. Title.

HD62.6 .L54 2000   00-008350
658'.048—dc21   CIP

9 8 7 6 5 4 3 2

The paper used in this publication meets minimum requirements of the American National Standard for Information Sciences—Permanence of Paper for Printed Library Materials: ANSI Z39.48-1984.

Typeset in Sabon

Composition by R. Lynn Rivenbark
Macon, Georgia

Printed by
Automated Graphic Services
White Plains, Maryland

Foreword

This is the first Center for Public Service report to focus exclusively on the nonprofit sector. As such, it confirms the center's concern for the condition of public work wherever it takes place, whether in traditional government agencies, nonprofit organizations, or the increasing number of private firms that deliver work for government under contracts and grants. As the logo of the Center for Public Service suggests, the United States now has a multisectored public service in which talent and responsibility move much more freely across once impenetrable boundaries.

This report starts with the simple conclusion that the nonprofit sector has never been under greater pressure to improve its organizational performance as part of this new public service. Its funders, be they governments, charitable foundations, or individual givers, have never seemed so insistent about economy and results, while its clients, be they communities or individuals, have never been more demanding about efficiency and responsiveness. *How* the nonprofit sector does its work is becoming almost as important to funders and clients as *what* the sector actually delivers by way of goods and services.

The problem is that there is virtually no agreement on just how nonprofits can improve. As in government and the private sector, a nonprofit reform exists for every ideology—for those who believe nonprofit agencies should mostly be left alone to do their work as they see fit or those who advocate greater public scrutiny of nonprofits, as well as those who want to see nonprofit agencies redesigned to be patterned after best practices in the private sector or those who maintain that the two sectors are, to rephrase a famous maxim, all fundamentally alike in all unimportant respects.[1]

Unfortunately, the reason for the many options is that the sector and its networks of consultants, management associations, and scholars are only beginning to develop the research base to know what reforms might work under which conditions. Indeed, they have only begun to accept the possibility that organization makes a difference in outcome. As Christine W. Letts, William P. Ryan, and Allen Grossman argue, "The nonprofit sector appears highly ambivalent about strengthening its organizations. On the one hand, everyone can agree that we need to take care of the organizations that are tackling difficult problems. On the other hand, deeply ingrained behaviors, public policy, funding systems, and the culture of nonprofit service itself have all led the sector to rely on virtually anything *but* organizational capacity as a foundation for lasting effectiveness."[2]

This lack of agreement has not stopped the tides, or philosophies, of nonprofit management reform from rising. To the contrary, it may actually invite an unhealthy competition between alternative reforms. Unwilling to acknowledge the importance of organization to their futures, let alone develop their own templates for excellence, nonprofit agencies allow the tides of reform to work their will with little protection. The nonprofit sector can always order the tides to cease, but to quote William Wordsworth's famous poem about Danish King Canute's demand, "Deaf will be the sea." The nonprofit sector can winnow the tides for good, harvesting good ideas where appropriate while returning the inappropriate to the sea, or it can be buffeted by one storm of reform after another, watching its core capacity erode as the rising tides wash ashore with greater force and frequency.

This report could not have been written without the support of the Aspen Institute's Nonprofit Sector Research Fund, which provided a small grant to support the author's writing time, nor could the Center for Public Service exist without the support of its funders, including grants from the Dillon Fund, Ford Foundation, and David and Lucile Packard Foundation, and individual gifts from an anonymous funder and James A. Johnson, chairman of the Brookings Institution board. The report was improved significantly by comments from Alan Abramson of the Nonprofit Sector Research Fund, Peter Frumkin of Harvard University's

John F. Kennedy School of Government, Barbara Kibbe of the Packard Foundation, and Melissa Stone of the University of Minnesota's Humphrey Institute of Public Affairs.

The views expressed here are those of the author and should not be ascribed to any of the persons acknowledged above or to the trustees, officers, or other staff members of the Brookings Institution.

MICHAEL H. ARMACOST
President

Washington, D.C.
March 2000

Contents

*Making
Nonprofits Work*

CHAPTER ONE

An Introduction to the Tides

The nonprofit sector has never been under greater pressure to improve. Despite two decades of phenomenal growth, the sector suffers from a general impression that it is less efficient and more wasteful than its government and private competitors. Even if the sector could prove that it has achieved "ordinary excellence," spending money wisely and producing measurable results as a natural by-product of organizational design, it faces a serious public relations problem among clients and funders alike.

If the growing inventory of research on nonprofit management reform is an indicator, the pressure for reform undoubtedly is rising. A simple amazon.com search for books on "nonprofits" in October 1999 produced more than thirteen hundred separate items, including *100 Best Nonprofits to Work For, The Non-Profit Internet Handbook, Tools for Innovators,* and *The 21st Century Nonprofit.* And the list appears to be growing by leaps and bounds, even as the number of research journals and newsletters has been growing at a seemingly parallel pace.[3]

Melissa M. Stone, Barbara Bigelow, and William Crittenden counted nineteen journals with at least some relevance to the sector in their 1999 study of strategic management in nonprofit organizations, including targeted journals such as *Nonprofit Management and Leadership* and *Nonprofit and Voluntary Sector Quarterly* (and its predecessor, *Journal of Voluntary Action Research*) and more general management journals such as *Academy of Management Journal, Organization Studies,* and *Public Administration Review.*[4] Throw in the *Journal of Policy Analysis and*

Management, which devoted an entire issue to the sector in the spring of 1998, along with *Voluntus*, an international journal on the sector, and a dozen or so specialized journals directed toward specific issue areas such as health, arts, social service, and economic development, or management topics such as tax policy, accounting standards, and personnel, and the sector can easily claim three dozen outlets for its research.

Sorting all the research and books into discrete management philosophies would be impossible, in part because they often mix and match ideas from a variety of reform traditions. At the same time, it would be surprising if the nonprofit sector had invented something new in the field of management reform. Although reform ideas adapt to the times and sectors, they tend to concentrate in predictable sets that can be traced back to the dawn of this Republic and beyond. There is truly nothing new under the sun by way of management reform.

Scholars have even found evidence of bureaucratic reform during the Roman occupation of ancient Egypt, including an ancient papyrus from a Roman officer complaining about the number of persons "who have invented titles for themselves, such as comptroller, secretary, or superintendent, whereby they procure no advantage to the Treasury but swallow up the profits. It has therefore become necessary for me to send you instructions to arrange a single superintendent of good standing to be chosen for each estate on the responsibility of the local municipal council, and to abolish all remaining officers, though the superintendent elected shall have power to choose two, or at most three, assistants."[5] So much for claims by business guru Michael Hammer that he invented organizational reengineering.[6] The papyrus is dated 288 A.D.

This is not to suggest that the tides, or philosophies, of reform produce the same ideas in every sector. Recommending reengineering for an overlayered bureaucracy is one thing, recommending it for organizations that have yet to be engineered or formalized in the first place is another. One can find elements of at least four familiar tides of reform rising in the nonprofit sector, each one carrying a somewhat separate history and ideology from the others: (1) scientific management, which is built upon a template of best practices that all nonprofit agencies should adopt; (2) liberation management, which places its faith in outcome measurement as the compass by which nonprofit agencies should guide themselves regardless of how they are configured; (3) war on waste, which seeks higher nonprofit performance through mergers, acquisitions, shared administrative services, co-location, and other cost-saving techniques largely culled from the private industry and reengineering (downsizing) of the past two decades; and (4) watchful eye, which puts its emphasis on exposing non-profit organizations to the sunshine of public disclosure as a fundamental disciplining tool.

Presented in a numbered list, the four tides appear separate. However, the philosophies are often linked in reform proposals. Thus, many of the scientifically minded standards that funders and nonprofit associations now use to evaluate and promote organizational effectiveness endorse outcomes measurement and transparency, while many of the recent calls for nonprofit reengineering are designed to concentrate nonprofit capacity around the more efficient production of outcomes. One can even argue that there are only two basic tides: a first that focuses primarily on efficiency, restructuring, rules, and standards, and a second that emphasizes transparency and oneness.[7] However, the search for improvement can be friendly or adversarial, rooted in a basic sense that the sector will do the right thing naturally or a more disquieting sense that the sector is mostly resistant to change. It is trust that converts the two tides into four.

Even though the four tides of reform often reinforce each other, they do offer very different starting points for the journey to ordinary excellence. Scientific management and liberation management both suggest that the nonprofit organization look inward for inspiration, starting its reform journey either with a top-to-bottom inventory of its internal systems (scientific management) or a strategic planning process designed to create a precise outcomes chain that places inputs, activities, outputs, and outcomes in their proper, and measurable, place (liberation management). In contrast, war on waste and watchful eye suggest that the nonprofit organization and its funders and clients look across a local delivery zone, starting the reform journey either with a mapping process designed to identify waste and duplication, as well as targets for capacity building (war on waste), or a process for exposing a group of nonprofits to greater review through publication of common data or development of an organizational rating or certification system.

These reform traditions clearly have parallels in other sectors. As I have written of the federal government, "Congress and the presidency have had little trouble passing reform measures over the years, moving almost effortlessly from one reform philosophy to another and back again, rarely questioning the contradictions and consequences of each separate act. If government is not getting better, it is most certainly not for a lack of legislation."[8] Unlike the federal government, however, where a half century of often contradictory reforms have created a dense sediment of bureaucratic inertia, and where the problem has not been too little reform but too much, the nonprofit sector is mostly at the beginning of its reform journey.

Luckily, the nonprofit sector still has the opportunity to sort through the reform philosophies before committing itself to any particular path. Although the sector has its own paragons of bureaucratic inertia, most of its organizations have yet to accrete the needless rules and endless layers that have made the federal government a prime target for downsizing and delayering. The sector need only note that many of the rules and layers that make the federal government so difficult to manage emerged in past efforts to make government work. The tides of management reform produced the civil service system and its impossibly complicated classification system (scientific management), the inspector general concept and its effort to create the "visible odium of deterrence" in every corner of government (war on waste), the administrative rulemaking process and its endless opportunities for delay (watchful eye), and a host of efforts to break free of all of the above (liberation management). There but for the grace of good fortune goes the nonprofit sector. Thus, the private sector's most important lessons on management reform may be on what to avoid, not adopt.

This warning to take care emerges from a simple reconnaissance of the dominant reform conversations within the nonprofit sector. Supported by the Aspen Institute's Nonprofit Sector Research Fund and limited to a three-month review, this report is based on confidential interviews with a handful of the leaders in nonprofit management reform, a detailed search of Internet sources, and a modest survey of state associations of nonprofit organizations. As such, it can be viewed only as a reconnaissance at long range. The findings suggest that the nonprofit sector has a remarkable opportunity to prevent the excesses and fadism that have dominated reform efforts in government and the private sector. That can be done, however, only by recognizing the limits of knowledge on what does and does not work in making organizations work. Much as government and private leaders promote the benefits of this idea or that, the reality is that reform is an expensive, often exhausting, undertaking. The first step on the reform journey should be taken with great care, lest it be taken over and over again.

This report offers that simple lesson in three parts. Chapter 2 assesses the current climate for reform, comparing the trends that are simultaneously nationalizing the pressure for reform, while localizing the capacity for progress. Chapter 3 examines the four tides of nonprofit reform in more detail, offering examples and caveats from the portfolio of recent experience. Chapter 4 starts with a discussion of the limits of knowledge in the general field of nonprofit management reform, then reports on a survey of state nonprofit associations to estimate the current strength of the four tides. Although all four tides are currently active in the nonprofit sector, liberation management and war on waste are at their peak. Chapter 5 concludes the report with recommendations for taming the tides.

Despite the warnings to go a bit slower in becoming champions of any particular reform, this report is not a defense for the status quo or standing pat. As the next chapter will show, the sector must get better, if only to show its funders and clients that it is still a reasonable investment in a much more competitive climate. But even as one embraces the call for continuous improvement, the limits of any given model of reform must be recognized. If history is any guide, the search for one best way to improve organizations will not be any more successful for the nonprofit sector than it has been for the myriad government agencies and private firms that embraced Frederick Taylor's mirage of an ordered organizational world only to drown in the sands of bureaucratic excess.[9] The nonprofit sector would do well to remind itself that the journey toward ordinary excellence can take many different paths.

CHAPTER TWO

The Climate for Reform

The nonprofit sector contains a remarkably diverse set of organizations. Its roughly 1.1 million organizations range from tiny, one-person organizations to massive university and health care operations, while its 10.2 million employees cover the panoply of professions, from social work to education, medicine, and the arts. For scholars such as Michael T. Hannan and John H. Freeman who ask why humankind has produced so many different organizations, the nonprofit sector is a good place to look for the answer.[10]

Viewed from a distance as a group of organizations, the nonprofit sector is composed of a large number of relatively small organizations, the vast majority of which employ fewer than one hundred people. But viewed from a distance as a work force, the vast majority of nonprofit employees are employed at a relatively small number of very large institutions. As a result, researchers must often choose between studying the majority of nonprofit organizations or the majority of nonprofit employees, the two of which rarely dwell in the same place.

Not surprisingly, drawing generalizations from any single study of the nonprofit sector is difficult. One the one hand, large nonprofit organizations can behave more like large corporations and government agencies than like small nonprofits, while small nonprofits can behave more like small businesses and town governments than their large nonprofit brethren. On the other, nonprofits in a given field such as the arts, education, health, and so forth may behave more like their private and governmental peers regardless of size than like nonprofits of a similar size in other fields. Important differences also are evident by location, leader-ship, and funding source, all of which make organizational comparisons difficult and generalizations risky. Readers are forewarned, therefore, that the following reconnaissance takes a very broad look at what is a very diverse sector. Although considerable evidence supports many of the assertions that follow, they should view this discussion of nonprofit man-agement reform as a starting point for reflection.

Unfortunately, too much of the contemporary conversation about non-profit management reform is designed to create national pressure on the sector as a whole, whether to measure outcomes, make information transparent, or impose standards of excellence. However well intentioned such efforts might be, they speak to a general conclusion that all non-profit organizations should be more alike than different.

As such, the pressure to improve may yet confirm what sociologists now call "institutional isomorphism," meaning the tendency of organizations in the same field to become more alike than different whether through coer-cion, professionalization, or a deeply felt desire to improve the sector.[11] Scholars who study isomorphism do not ask why there are so many differ-ent kinds of organizations, but why there are so few. Their answer is that organizations tend to become more like each other over time, particularly when they share a common environment that includes like-minded funders such as Congress. Reformers should be careful what they wish. To the extent they seek organizations that look and feel the same, they may weaken the organizational diversity they so often celebrate.

Before examining the pressures that are pushing nonprofit organiza-tions to be more alike in management, taking an inventory of the state of the sector at the twentieth century's end would be useful. Despite the gen-eral absence of performance measures, the sense "out there" is that the sector is in need of dramatic reshaping and reform.

The State of the Sector

The past two decades have witnessed the best of times and worst of times for the nonprofit sector. Government funding fell, then rose; public con-fidence rose, then fell, and has only started to rise again; the nonprofit labor market expanded, but so did organizational stress and turnover. Where the sector stands today depends on which indicator one chooses.

Start with the good news on growth. Measured in private dollars, the nonprofit sector has never been richer. Private contributions increased by

16 percent in 1998, marking the seventh consecutive year that funding has gone up.[12] Although contributions to educational institutions grew the fastest, all nonprofits appeared to flourish with the continued economic boom. With $1.2 billion in cash and in-kind contributions, the Salvation Army was ranked as the number one fund-raiser in the Independent Sector's 1999 review.

Measured in government dollars, the sector has also been growing, albeit in relatively small increments each year. Compared with the early 1980s, government is still far behind what it once gave; but measured against the early 1990s, government grants and contracts to nonprofit agencies are headed in what most in the sector would agree is the right direction. At the same time, the nonprofit sector has been reducing its dependence on fees for services slightly each year. Although fees for service continue to grow in absolute terms, they have been shrinking as a percentage of total nonprofit revenue.

Finally, measured in total employment, the sector has never been bigger. Although the sector has been growing for nearly three decades, the curve is clearly accelerating. From 1972 to 1982, the sector grew roughly 200,000 jobs per year, increasing from 4.6 million full- and part-time jobs to 6.5 million. Much of that growth is in health care, which added 1.1 million jobs, and social services, which more than doubled from 450,000 jobs to nearly a million.[13] But from 1982 to 1996, the sector jumped by almost 300,000 a year to 10.2 million, a net increase of almost 4 million jobs driven by rising contributions and a surge in revenue.[14] Lacking more precise data, it is impossible to know exactly how much of the increased revenue went to cover new employees, but the trend lines suggest an obvious link.

The nonprofit sector left the 1990s much better off than it entered, prompting Independent Sector president Sara Meléndez to declare the glass half full: "By all accounts our sector is enjoying good health and vitality. Furthermore, foundations have been making record-breaking grants, corporations have increased their giving, and so have households. America is richer than ever. In fact, we're richer than any country has ever been."[15]

The glass is certainly half full, if not fuller, for researchers, degree-granting programs, and students interested in nonprofit careers. For example, research on the sector is growing. The number of journals is up, attendance at research conferences appears to be rising, and the number of articles and papers of interest to nonprofit organizations has surely increased. Thus, Stone, Bigelow, and Crittenden were able to identify a total of sixty-six articles over the past two decades that focus specifically on nonprofit strategic management—twenty-one that focus on nonprofit strategy formulation, twenty-four on strategy content, and twenty-one on strategy implementation. One of the articles was published in the 1970s, twenty-six in the 1970s, and thirty-nine in the 1990s, suggesting an increase in research productivity or a growing interest in strategic planning.

The number of degree-granting programs has also increased. According to an ongoing census by Roseanne Mirabella, a principal investigator in the *Nonprofit Management Education in the Year 2000* study, the number of graduate management programs with a nonprofit concentration (three or more courses) grew from just seventeen in 1990 to seventy-six by 1997. Roughly two-fifths of the nonprofit concentrations were in schools of public policy and administration, another sixth each in schools of business or social work, and the final quarter scattered throughout other schools.[16]

Finally, interest in careers in nonprofit organizations is up. Simply stated, the nonprofit sector has become a destination of choice for graduates of the nation's top public policy and administration graduate schools. Recent graduates of the top schools were twice as likely as members of earlier classes to take their first jobs in the nonprofit sector, and they have shown surprising interest in the private sector. In all, just over half of recent graduates started their public service careers outside government, with the nonprofit sector gaining the greatest ground against government. Twenty-five percent of members of the class of 1993 took their first postgraduate job in the nonprofit sector, more than double the proportion among their peers in the classes of 1973 and 1974 (see table 2-1).

The nonprofit sector is popular in part because government is not. Government is still seen among all graduates as the sector most likely to represent the public interest but has come to trail both the private and nonprofit sectors on spending money wisely and helping people. Although where the graduates sit in their current jobs influences what they think of the three sectors, government has lost the confidence of even some of its own recruits. Government employees may still think their sector is the best place to represent the public interest, but they no longer believe their sector is the best place to help people or spend money wisely. Given the nearly uniform commitment to helping people among these

Table 2-1. First Postgraduate Job and Current Job

Percent

Job location	Classes of 1973 and 1974 (N = 200)		Classes of 1978 and 1979 (N = 231)		Class of 1983 (N = 171)		Class of 1988 (N = 192)		Class of 1993 (N = 196)	
	First job	Current job	First job	Current job	First job	Current job	First job	Current job	First job	Current job
Government	76	50	62	46	68	51	55	39	49	41
Private Sector	11	28	21	38	21	30	21	32	23	26
Nonprofit Sector	12	15	15	12	12	15	23	25	25	28

graduates, this is arguably the absolute worst position facing government as it struggles to compete for talent.

Alas, there is plenty of bad news on the state of the nonprofit sector, too. The nonprofit sector has never been under greater stress, as evidenced by doubts about its performance and ethical conduct. Federal budget cuts and private competition have affected already thin operating margins, while the highly publicized United Way and Salt Lake City Olympics scandals have sparked a broad debate about the effectiveness and legitimacy of nonprofit organizations. According to Lester M. Salamon, budget cuts "not only increase the need for nonprofit services; they also reduce the ability of nonprofit organizations to meet these needs." At the same time, private competition has led many nonprofits to start charging for services, which Salamon argues "has put a squeeze on some of the 'mission-related' activities that have made nonprofits distinctive (e.g., charity care, research, training) and raised questions about the nonprofit form."

Similar to the effort to become more like private businesses, this growing dependence on fee-for-service funding has provoked hard questions about the sector's overall mission, which Salamon describes as a "reaction against what some see as the over-professionalization of human services and the lack of adequate performance measures and accountability mechanisms in the nonprofit sector," thereby creating "a growing mismatch between the way the sector actually operates and the quaint nineteenth-century image that dominates public understanding."[17]

How this "crisis of legitimacy," as Salamon labels it, has affected public confidence is not clear, in part because the survey data are so shallow. Beyond the Independent Sector/Gallup biennial polls, which ask only the most basic questions about confidence, virtually no data are available on how Americans form their opinions of the sector and whether they have any real basis for judging performance and accountability. This is not to discount the good news from recent Independent Sector polls. The number of Americans who believe that charitable organizations have become more effective over the past five years in providing services is up slightly from 1994 to 1999, as is the number who say that charitable organizations play an important role in speaking out on important issues and in making communities better places to live.[18]

Rather, the gains are modest at best and within sampling error on all but the role of charitable organizations in making communities better. Meanwhile, the number of Americans who say that the need for charitable organizations has grown over the past five years and that charities are honest and ethical in their use of donated funds are both down since 1994. In other words, the data suggest that the nonprofit sector has treaded water during the 1990s, even as volunteerism continues to rise, especially among young Americans.[19]

Nor is it clear how the crisis has affected those who work and volunteer in the sector, again because so little information is available. The only data I have found on this topic come from my 1999 book *The New Public Service,* which is based on a random sample survey of one thousand graduates of the nation's top public policy and administration graduate programs. Asked which sector they trusted most to deliver services on the public's behalf, the graduates ranked government first at 42 percent, nonprofit organizations second at 29 percent, and private contractors third at 17 percent.

When the graduates were asked about specific jobs, the sectors divided more clearly. When asked which sector was best at helping people, the graduates rated nonprofits first at 52 percent, with government second at 30 percent, and private contractors trailing far behind at just 6 percent. But when asked which sector was best at spending money wisely, private contractors emerged on top at 38 percent, nonprofits second at 33 percent, and government at just 15 percent. Government was first at 59 percent when the graduates were asked which sector was best at representing the public interest, followed by nonprofits at 26 percent, and private contractors at just 5 percent. Even graduates who were working for private firms at the time of the survey had no illusions about their sector. They saw the private sector as tops at just one thing, spending money wisely.[20]

Once again, the good news contains cause for concern. With each successive class, graduates who are currently working in the nonprofit sector have become less confident in the ability of their own sector to help people. Whereas 70 percent of classes that graduated in the 1970s rated their sector as the best at helping people, only 54 percent of classes in the 1990s agreed.

Moreover, the number of graduates currently working the sector who said they trusted their own organizations to do the right thing all of the time or just about always also tumbled, from 54 percent in classes from the 1970s to 40 percent in classes from the 1990s. It is not clear whether the more recent recruits will become more confident as they move up their relatively flat organizations and have more contact with the people their organizations help. It is clear, however, that there is a potential generation gap among older and young nonprofit employees that deserves watching.

The Pressure to Improve

Whether the sector's glass is half full or half empty, a nearly unanimous consensus has emerged that nonprofit organizations have to improve their performance. Much of the "lean and mean" rhetoric that so pre-occupied private firms and government agencies during the 1980s and early 1990s has now filtered over to the nonprofit sector.

The tides of nonprofit reform clearly existed well before the current crisis of legitimacy, however. One need only page back through old issues of *Harvard Business Review, Chronicle of Philanthropy, Nonprofit Times, Administration in Social Work, Journal of Voluntary Action Research,* or *Journal of Policy Analysis and Management* to spot the rise and fall of many ideas regarding reform, all of which have been hot at one time or another in corporate America.

What may make the current period different for the nonprofit sector is the intensity of the reform pressure. Individual nonprofits have little choice but to show improvement, whether by learning the language of reform or by implementing change. "However the struggle between providers ultimately plays out," writes William P. Ryan in his assessment of the new landscape for nonprofits, "the nonprofit sector cannot return to a halcyon time when charities were 'uncontaminated' by the market. . . . Indeed, nonprofits are now forced to reexamine their reasons for existing in light of a market that rewards discipline and performance and emphasizes organizational capacity rather than for-profit or nonprofit status and mission. Nonprofits have no choice but to reckon with these forces—forces that were unleashed and that continue to be shaped not by the private sector but by government itself."[21]

The competition is here to stay. Having entered the traditional human service market with significant investments of corporate capital, national firms such as Lockheed Martin IMS and Maximus have no intention of leaving any time soon. To the contrary, they likely intend to expand their market share, whether by assuming government functions through privatization and outsourcing or by displacing nonprofits as the providers of choice in traditional contract activities.[22]

Nonprofits also face increased competition from each other. It is a point well made by Burton A. Weisbrod in 1998. His evidence is not limited merely to the "skyrocketing user fees" he finds at nonprofit colleges, hospitals, museums, and zoos. "Nonprofits are engaging in an increasing array of new, ancillary activities designed to raise money," he argues, in the process "emulating private firms, finding ways to attract more 'customers' and donors. Prospective contributors are being treated increasingly as objects of psychological analysis in order to discover their motivations."[23] The nonprofit sector may be setting yearly records in total revenues, reaching $625 billion in 1998, but so are the private contractors who work at the state and local levels of government, meaning that the competition for resources can only increase. In San Diego County, California, Catholic Charities is competing for a share of the welfare-to-work market against two private firms, Lockheed Martin IMS and Maximus, and the remnants of the San Diego County human services department. But it could just as easily have been Maximus against the Young Men's Christian Association (YMCA) or Goodwill Industries, all of which are competing to deliver services in Milwaukee County, Wisconsin.

The nonprofit sector has made impressive gains in competing for graduates of the top public policy and administration schools, and it has clearly become a destination of choice for many talented students. But whether nonprofit agencies can continue to outbid the private sector by offering the psychic income of altruism and mission is anyone's guess. Major consulting firms such as Deloitte & Touche and Andersen Consulting are currently offering top public policy graduates $65,000–$75,000 starting salaries and $5,000–$10,000 signing bonuses. To students packing $40,000–$50,000 in college loans, the private sector offers an oasis of relief that the nonprofit sector and its funders have yet to replicate.

Nonprofits have many choices in competing for resources and talent in this more unforgiving climate. They can hunker down and hope that private firms fail miserably in delivering service and give the responsibilities back, which is an entirely wistful strategy that ignores the substantial success that Lockheed Martin IMS and others have shown in delivering welfare-to-work services. Nonprofits can also privatize portions of themselves or enter into partnerships with private firms, both of which can so fundamentally alter their mission that Ryan warns "nonprofits may conclude that winning isn't everything."[24]

The obvious alternative is for nonprofits to become more effective and disciplined in what they already do, whether to prepare themselves for possible partnerships of the kind Lockheed Martin IMS now oversees in Dade County, Florida, or to gird themselves for a leaner, meaner funding environment. Hence, the explosion in how-to books on how nonprofits can become more businesslike. Yet, even though good reasons can be cited for nonprofits to become more effective in their work, not the least of which is the obligation to spend money wisely, the sector may still lose the competition. As Peter Frumkin and Alice Andre-Clark argue, "Non-profits can never win an efficiency battle with for-profit firms in the welfare to work arena. Any attempt to compete with the 'new corporate social workers' will lead to an efficiency-driven race to the bottom, which nonprofit organizations are ill equipped to win."[25]

Moreover, there can be such a thing as too much reform. Decades of flotsam and jetsam from the tides of federal government reform have produced a kind of fatigue in which agencies and their employees sag at the latest proposal, sure that this, too, shall pass like the waves at a seashore. The statute books are filled with examples of ideas that agencies either could not or would not implement for a lack of resources and presidential leadership, while surveys of federal employees suggest a shallow embrace at best of Vice President Al Gore's aggressive, yet eerily familiar, "reinventing government" campaign.[26]

My survey for *The New Public Service* suggests that the nonprofit sector may already be approaching a certain saturation point for reform. Asked how many times they had changed their work as a result of a reform effort such as reinventing or total quality management (TQM), more than half of the graduates currently working in the nonprofit sector answered once or more, including a fifth who answered that they had been asked to change their approach to work four or more times.[27] Although the graduates currently working in government faced an even higher level of reinventing (two-thirds had experienced reinventing at least once), there appears to be more reform underway in the nonprofit sector than one might have guessed from books such as *Reengineering Your Nonprofit Organization*, which offers the "fundamental redesign of a nonprofit's organizational structure, processes, service delivery mechanism, and technology" as the antidote to the "pain" that Alceste T. Pappas believes most nonprofits currently feel.[28]

Apparently, at least some of that pain may have been caused by reinventing. Of the graduates whose nonprofits had been reinvented, only 14 percent said the effort had made things much better in their workplace; 39 percent said somewhat better; 10 percent, somewhat worse; 7 percent, much worse; and 26 percent, the reform had not made a difference one way or the other. Not surprisingly perhaps, graduates who have been through multiple reinventings were less satisfied with their current jobs and less likely to recommend a career in public service to others than graduates who had been reinvented once or less.

Despite all the warnings about reform, the pressure to get better is unlikely to abate and the number of reform efforts is unlikely to decline. To the contrary, the reform pressure seems to be increasing for the nonprofit sector. All the pieces are in place: growing demand from funders, rising expectations from clients, increased pressure from advocates both inside the sector and outside, burgeoning competition from other providers also both inside and outside the sector, and an apparent explosion in the number of organizational consultants ready to help the nonprofit sector identify problems and implement solutions.

If the government reform movement is any guide, the nonprofit sector could be in for a very long storm, with all that means for administrative stress in perhaps the most thinly staffed of the three sectors currently engaged in delivering public goods and services on the public's behalf. The federal government has been involved in one reform effort after another for the better part of the twentieth century, starting with Theodore Roosevelt's appointment of the first of a long list of blue-ribbon reform commissions in 1907 and ending with thirty years of nearly nonstop reinventing by Republicans and Democrats alike. Unfortunately, little evidence supports the claim that government has gotten better because of any particular reform impulse. Government probably has gotten better mostly in spite of the reforms, if it has gotten better at all. Technology, professionalization, natural learning, and the simple passage of time may have more to do with any gains in productivity than the uneven application of reinventing, reengineering, scientific management, war on waste, and so forth.

The climate for reform is shaped by more than a generalized sense of need, however. At least two countervailing pressures—one national in character, the other local—suggest the tides of nonprofit reform can only intensify. Even as national forces increase the pressure to improve, thereby raising the "temperature of the ocean" as one respondent interviewed for this project described it, local realities limit the ability of individual nonprofits to design and implement reasonable first steps based on the best available knowledge. Simply stated, the temperature of the ocean may be rising, but individual agencies still pay attention to a relatively small number of big fish, or so the respondent argues. To the extent those big fish do not recognize the limits of knowledge, the result could be several decades of wasted motion instead of thoughtful reform that might move the nonprofit sector closer to ordinary excellence.

Nationalizing Trends

Management reform was hardly the only response that the nonprofit sector could have made to a changing climate. Nonprofits could have joined together and raised the millions to mount the kind of public education campaign that appears to have had such a dramatic impact on public confidence in the military, for example.[29] Or they could have joined in the kind of lobbying campaign that private contractors have used so successfully to promote the outsourcing of federal jobs through such statutes as the 1998 Federal Activities Inventory Reform Act, which requires all federal entities to provide lists of jobs that might be eligible for privatization.[30] They even could have joined together in loose collaborations to reduce administrative costs, integrate information, and organize public support from the grass roots.

The nonprofit sector did a bit of all three; the only problem was that the level of effort was mostly so modest that the impacts could only be minimal. The sector has never had the dollars to mount a sustained public relations campaign and has been reluctant to use its lobbying and organizing authorities for fear of a congressional backlash. The sector did mount a successful effort to defeat Oklahoma Republican representative Ernest Istook's 1996 antilobbying legislation but has long worried that full exercise of its lobbying freedom might provoke just such legislation. Ironically, the sector has mostly protected its lobbying and organizing freedom by not using it.

WHY MANAGEMENT BECAME THE ANSWER. Others have written with more acuity about why management reform became the answer to the question of how to make nonprofits work. Frumkin and Andre-Clark argue that private competition led some nonprofits to believe they must fight entrepreneurial fire with fire, even as funders and scholars began to coalesce around management reform as a path to accountability.

Consider, for example, how business school professor J. Gregory Dees suggests nonprofits prepare to "sail commercial waters": "If nonprofits are to explore commercial options, it is essential both that they build business capabilities and that they manage organizational culture. Management skills are important for all nonprofit organizations, but commercialization calls for expertise, knowledge, and attitudes more commonly found in the business world. Nonprofit managers need to become trained in business methods if they are to explore commercial options effectively."[31] Presumably, business schools, not public policy and administration programs, would be the place to go for the training.

Frumkin and Andre-Clark also point to the more general professionalization of the nonprofit sector as a driver for management improvement: "Many professionals want to bring a new rigor to their work and develop standards to measure their performance, as a basis both for their own advancement within the field and for the development of a body of expert knowledge. Reengineering, TQM, and benchmarking are appealing because they help justify the move from volunteer labor to well compensated professional staffing."[32]

This professionalization is a classic form of what sociologists label "normative isomorphism" in which certain practices become part of the conventional wisdom of what a good organization or manager does. As Frumkin and Mark T. Kim argue, this professionalization tracks closely with basic changes in the world of institutional philanthropy, not the least of which is the rise of project grants, which have come to outnumber general operating grants by a ratio of close to 3 to 1, and the parallel professionalization of grantmaking staffs: "The greater level of oversight and heightened emphasis on effectiveness and efficiency have necessitated the recruitment and training of program staff who know not only how to provide services but also to handle donors and the new rigors of securing contributed income. This has led to an even greater emphasis on fundraising skills within the sector and to the rising salaries of development professionals."[33]

Graduates of the top public policy and administration schools who start their careers in the nonprofit sector carry more than commitment with them. They also carry ideas for improvement, including new techniques for managerial reform. Many also carry subscriptions to the *Harvard Business Review*, which has become a prime destination for scholarship on nonprofit reform. Although the journal has accepted a reasonable range of articles on nonprofit reform, including work on venture philanthropy and what nonprofits can occasionally teach for-profits, its primary focus has been on how nonprofits can become more like for-profits, which itself reveals a nationalizing trend of a sort.[34] In 1996, for example, V. Kasturi Rangan and colleagues in May wrote about doing better at doing good, Joanne Scheff and Philip Kotler in October wrote of marketing solutions for arts organizations, and Alan Andreasen in November wrote about how nonprofits can find for-profit partners—all important contributions to the nonprofit literature, but all endorsing management reform as the primary solution to problems in the sector.[35]

More important for the tides of nonprofit reform, graduates who start out in the nonprofit sector are buffeted by at least three nationalizing trends that by accident or intent make their organizations look more alike than different, particularly through common management practices. First, national funding organizations have started to embrace specific management reforms as a precondition for funding. Second, the Internet has created the opportunity for national competition over what used to be local funding. Third, the rise of a new public service characterized by high levels of sector switching has produced more opportunity for the spread of managerial best practices even where there is little proof of effectiveness.

THE NATIONALIZATION OF REFORM. One way nonprofit organizations become more alike is through efforts to impose national standards, whether embodied in federal law such as the Uniform Management of Institutional Funds Act or through grantmaking practices. Although Peter Dobkin Hall correctly notes that such reforms are notoriously difficult to implement, he also argues that "uniform standards are both symptomatic of the powerful forces that have been transforming nonprofit enterprise and, in themselves, potent sources of transformation."[36]

Consider the United Way of America's decision to embrace outcomes measurement as an example of the power of such efforts to reshape the nonprofit debate. Its adoption of a single management reform reflects a nationalization of reform pressure that is occurring throughout the sector, whether in financial management, fund-raising, or training.

The trend is simple: not only are national organizations such as the United Way of America endorsing the broad effort to improve, but they also are now putting their substantial weight behind specific reform ideas, to the point of providing the technical assistance and reform templates needed for implementation. Even acknowledging that fads and fashions in management reform were evident long before the United Way of America appointed its Task Force on Impact in 1995, the heavy investment in outcomes measurement marked the first time a national organization had so boldly advocated for a specific management reform. Hence, the United Way of America website includes a long list of publications designed to teach local United Ways and nonprofits how to focus on outcomes the United Way way.

The United Way of America investment is obvious in the number and quality of the organization's instruction on how to focus on results. Its *Measuring Program Outcomes: A Practical Approach* is arguably the best available instructional guide on outcomes-based management. With chapters from why organizations should measure outcomes to analyzing and reporting outcomes, and primary materials on challenges from setting time lines for planning and implementing reform to a sample pledge of confidentiality from data collectors, the document provides careful guidance to any organization about to start the outcomes journey. And its appendix on issues in developing data collection instruments and procedures, which includes a sample rating scale for trained observer ratings of a playground for preschool children, could easily be used in an introductory methods course as an exemplar of how to teach basic research design.[37]

The manual also includes a glossary of terms that provides enough information so that any organization, however shallowly committed to the cause, could write a compelling outcomes plan. Accompanied by a twenty-three-minute video and a *Measuring Program Outcomes Training Kit,* the entire package represents a significant investment in the technical assistance needed to push outcomes management well down into the non-profit sector. Although the kit is more useful perhaps to local United Ways that wish to teach, instruct, or even coerce their grantees into building an outcomes system, no one can read through the materials or watch the videotape and not be impressed by the United Way of America's firm embrace of outcomes measurement as an essential component of a well-running nonprofit.

The history of the effort offers little insight on why the United Way of America embraced outcomes measurement. On the one hand, the organization most certainly concluded that focusing on outcomes can help its local organizations evaluate competing proposals and ensure donor confidence. On the other hand, focusing on results allowed the United Way of America to confront public concerns about accountability following the resignation of its president, William Aramony, who was convicted of defrauding the organization of $1 million. But whatever the blend of legitimate concern and political pressure, the United Way of American entered the reform movement with gale force, issuing policy papers, authoring measurement manuals, promoting implementation, and generally cheerleading its local associates to adopt outcomes measurement as an allocation tool. By mid-1998, roughly three hundred local United Ways were either considering or using an outcomes measurement system.

The United Way of America is hardly the only national organization to support reform, however. The Benton Foundation has established a broad initiative to strengthen the technological capacity of the nonprofit sector and exploit the power of the Internet. Easily reachable at helping.org, America Online's new "one-stop resource for giving and volunteering," the Resources for Nonprofits Partnership, explains its mission in simple terms:

Designed by nonprofits for nonprofits, this area of helping.org is a starting point for nonprofits that are interested in learning the most effective ways to use online technology, from recruiting volunteers and more effectively supporting a membership, to using it as an advocacy tool. Recognizing the value of the many existing efforts of nonprofit technology assistance providers and exemplary technology uses by nonprofits throughout the nation, this section aggregates and annotates information, tools, resources and ideas, and provides the guidance needed to integrate digital, interactive technology into nonprofits' programs. You will also find here examples of effective ways that nonprofits are using online communications tools to further their missions. While focused on the use of online communications, the Resources for Nonprofits Partnership also links to online clearinghouses of other nonprofit resources, such as information about the sector, management assistance, news and jobs.[38]

Although both efforts are national in scope, the Benton Foundation and United Way of America initiatives are different in the level of implied enforcement. Visitors can peruse the Benton Foundation's "online toolkit" as they please, clicking down the links to pick up new skills on planning a website, fund-raising on the Internet, finding computer help, or enhancing the way they work with computer technology.

In contrast, the United Way of America is unrelenting about its ultimate goal to convert the nonprofit sector to its image of outcomes management. The central indicator of its success will be nothing less than the adoption of outcomes measurement by every last one of its local partners, and, in turn, their use of outcomes measurement to make all funding decisions. It is a precedent-setting goal, marking one of the first times a national funder has so clearly committed itself and its partners to a single management reform as the sine qua non of effectiveness. Other national organizations such as the National Center for Nonprofit Boards and Independent Sector have committed themselves to broad improvement, but none of the majors has ever put so much weight behind one reform.

Just how many funders will follow suit is not clear. Outcomes measurement is already beginning to fade at the federal level and has been only marginally effective in the states. But funders have enormous influence over nonprofit management practices. As they sort through their own agenda of best practices for grantmaking, they are likely to embrace reforms that will percolate downward to their grantees.

Although many of the ideas for better evaluation, collaboration, and learning now circulating throughout the foundation community make eminent sense for the nonprofit sector as a whole, foundations would do well to read Thomas E. Backer's 1999 analysis of their own innovations: "Even if an innovation is truly relevant to improving philanthropic practice, it will not likely do so unless there is adequate *time* (most significant change takes more time than we would like to think!) and *money* (significant change is usually expensive to produce!). A kind of 'field triage' may be needed to pick the innovations most worth pursuing, so that energies can be concentrated on those few with the greatest chance for survival and impact."[39] If a national foundation cannot implement a learning or collaboration model, what chance does a small nonprofit have?

THE NATIONALIZATION OF GIVING. One reason local nonprofits might be listening to national reforms is the growing realization that the local ties that once bound local givers to their communities are starting to break down. Hence, the second nationalizing trend that might lead nonprofits to become more alike than different involves the rise of Internet-based search-and-giving engines. Although individual nonprofits have used the Internet to reach potential donors for several years, individual donors did not have the option to search the nation for giving targets until October 1999, when America Online (AOL) and the Tides Foundation entered the fund-sorting business.

America Online launched first with helping.org, a multilevel site that includes a powerful search-and-giving engine that was developed in partnership with GuideStar, an arm of Philanthropic Research Inc., a nonprofit information provider. Whereas AOL contributes enormous Internet access and brand identity, GuideStar contributes information via a vast database built around the Internal Revenue Service (IRS) Business Master

File, IRS Form 990 and 990 EZ that almost all (501)(c)(3) tax-exempt charitable organizations must file each year.

The combination of technological savvy and information yields an extraordinarily deep, sometimes overwhelming, inventory of options. Visitors to helping.org can volunteer for service by searching through local organizations by size, ZIP code, interest area, distance from home, and level of commitment (one-time or continuing), or they can donate money by searching through GuideStar's entire directory of 620,000 non-profit organizations by size, ZIP code, and interest area. Once visitors finish their "volunteer here" search, they can forward their name and address to selected organizations with a single click. It is then up to the organizations to make contact.

The "donate now" search is just as simple but produces three levels of information. A first click produces a brief template of GuideStar summary information that makes an organization's who-we-are/what-we-do pitch for support, along with a snippet of financial information. A second click produces a deeper inventory of information, including long paragraphs on mission statement and goals, programs and results, financials, and leaders. A third click produces an even thicker report that includes the chief executive's biography, a list of objectives for the coming year, and a full-blown financial assessment built around the Form 990 categories. Visitors are also free to pivot easily in and out of the site to visit every organization's own website.

Two features of the site are particularly important for the nationalization of management reform. The first is the use of an outcomes language to help donors sort eligible organizations. Helping.org does not make outcomes judgments itself. Instead, it merely gives access to the GuideStar files, which contain the outcomes information. Although a cursory inspection of the outcomes information supplied by individual nonprofits suggests that nonprofits have some way to go toward embracing a shared definition of outcomes (most of the ones I sampled would be defined as activities), helping.org is promoting a particular vision of how nonprofits should measure themselves in a competitive funding environment. Presumably, donors should prefer organizations that at least try to measure outcomes, even if they do a poor job.

The second feature of helping.org is the sheer onslaught of unmediated information. To embrace the tides metaphor, accessing helping.org is like being hit by a category five hurricane. Even with helpful prompts, the search engine produces dozens of possibilities for both volunteering and donating. Although helping.org does provide links to the national Council of Better Business Bureaus and the National Charities Information Bureau, both of which provide ratings of a small subset of the total database, the visitor is left to his or her devices for working down the alphabetized lists and can only muse at the future of a sector populated by organizations that rename themselves just to get higher in the alphabet.

Giveforchange.com solves the information overload through a partnership between eGrants.org, a subsidiary of the Tides Foundation, a San Francisco-based nonprofit intermediary, and Working Assets Online, a subsidiary of Working Assets Funding Services, a socially progressive provider of long-distance services. The site is unabashed about its comparative strength: "Welcome to Giveforchange, the best place on the web to find nonprofit groups working for social change. We make it easy for you to make a difference."

Unlike helping.org, giveforchange.com does not admit just anyone to its inventory of organizations. The website only lists organizations that have survived a winnowing process that focuses explicitly on mission. According to the selection policy posted at giveforchange.com, groups must work in one of eleven issue areas (children and families, civil rights, economic justice, environment, gay and lesbian rights, health care, international relief, media and freedom of expression, Northern California, peace and human rights, and rights and welfare of animals), have existed as an organization for at least a year, and fit under the eGrants.org mission statement: "Promotes change towards a healthy society, one which is founded on principles of social justice, broadly shared economic opportunity, a robust democratic process, and sustainable environmental practices. eGrants.org believes that healthy societies rely fundamentally on respect for human rights, the vitality of communities and a celebration of diversity."

Like helping.org, donors have one-click access to a wide range of giving options sorted by the eleven issue areas, location, and size. However, they also have the option to search the inventory of roughly four hundred qualifying organizations by eleven change strategies: advocacy, education, direct service, grass roots, litigation, training, monitoring, investigation, project development, research, and regranting. A first click produces a simple page outlining a given organization's mission and methodology. Beyond the option to pivot in and out to each organization's website, donors receive no other information—nothing on program size, results, leaders, or financials. Donors have to trust that giveforchange.com has done its due diligence on the financials and trust that mission and methodology are all that matters.

Whether the organizational information is mediated or not, both helping.org and giveforchange.com offer a glimpse of a radical future in which donors are largely separated from their localities in making the giving decision. Although visitors are free to search for giving opportunities by ZIP code or geography, the two websites promote a more comprehensive approach in which savvy givers find the best organization for their views. Helping.org allows visitors to create an inventory of what it labels "helping favorites," while giveforchange.com keeps track of giving decisions under "giving basket." The parallels to amazon.com and other web-based shopping sites are unmistakable and deliberate.

The question is how this nationalization affects the pressure to improve. Both sites encourage nonprofits to focus more on mission. Both sites also tend to favor nonprofits with Internet websites, though one could argue that givers who visit helping.org or giveforchange.com were predisposed to think of Internet access as a measure of effectiveness. Where the two sites depart is in the value placed on specific management reforms. Like the United Way of America, helping.org embraces outcomes measurement, as well as clean financial statements. Each donor search produces four alphabetized lists: a first list containing all organizations with complete and recent GuideStar information, a second containing all organizations with current financials only, a third with old GuideStar information, and a fourth with all the rest.

Because helping.org only displays the first thirty-five organizations on a given search, the incentives to provide the kind of information GuideStar needs are obvious. As GuideStar notes in its instructions to participating nonprofits, "The GuideStar database includes basic listings on all 501(c)(3) organizations. However, the best way to attract potential donors is to enhance your basic GuideStar listing with additional information about your mission, objectives, beneficiaries, etc." Whatever they do in implementing outcomes measurement, nonprofits would be wise to learn the GuideStar language. Otherwise, their best option is to change their names to start with the letter *a*.

Ironically, GuideStar's success may weaken the effectiveness of the United Way of America's outcomes campaign. The more GuideStar empowers individual donors to choose, the more United Ways across the country are pressured to provide the same choice in their annual giving campaigns, which in turn reduces the authority to use outcomes for making funding decisions.

As with all of the reform efforts discussed in this report, it is too early to know whether helping.org or giveforchange.com will alter giving patterns. Working Assets launched the site with a $1 million dollar match, which would imagine a $2 million payout during the first year of operation, hardly a stunning figure. Nevertheless, it is impossible to ignore the potential for change embodied in Internet-based fundgiving. Who would have guessed five years ago that Jeff Bezos, chief executive officer of amazon.com, would be *Time* magazine's person of the year in 1999? Internet fundgiving creates a new playing field for a national competition that will surely make nonprofits more alike than different, not the least of which are their advertising efforts and outcomes language.

THE NATIONALIZATION OF TALENT. The third trend affecting the tides of reform involves the emergence of a multisectored public service characterized by high levels of sector switching. Gone is the thirty-year government-centered public service of the 1960s and 1970s. Public servants now move freely across the sectors in search of challenging work, the chance to accomplish something worthwhile, and the opportunity to advance.

My research on graduates of the top public policy and administration schools suggests that sector switching is a defining characteristic of the new public service. If intentions hold true, recent graduates of the nation's top public policy and administration schools will change jobs and sectors at a record rate. Convinced that it is unwise to spend too much time with any one employer, the classes of 1988 and 1993 were already ahead of their well-traveled older peers at the five-year mark. Although those intentions may change as classes age, the data discussed below suggest that today's graduates have already accepted the multisector public service as their career reality. Consider four broad pieces of evidence on the intention to switch.

—Asked whether they thought they would stay in their current sector for the rest of their career or switch sectors at some point, roughly two-fifths of the graduates said they intended to switch. The greatest intention to switch came from graduates who were in the private sector at the time of the interviews (47 percent), while the lowest came from those in local government (26 percent).

—Asked how many years a person should stay with any given employer before moving on, 27 percent of the graduates said less than five years, 30 percent said five to ten years, and just 5 percent said more than ten years. The rest either did not know how long a person should stay (36 percent) or refused to answer (2 percent).

—Asked whether they were doing the kind of work today that they would like to be doing five years from now, 62 percent of the graduates said yes, with virtually no difference across the three sectors or between federal, state, and local government. As with the other findings, the numbers declined over the five classes. Whereas 69 percent of the classes of 1973 and 1974 felt settled in, only 55 percent of the class of 1993 agreed. The fact that the decline was not steeper suggests that the question may have tapped into more of a hypothetical longing about the future rather than a clear readiness to move.

—Asked to imagine alternative career destinations through the simple phrase "if you could choose," and asked whether they would rather work for government, a private business, or a nonprofit organization, 63 percent of the graduates picked the sector they were already in. Roughly a fifth of the graduates who were currently working for government said they would rather work for a private business (10 percent) or nonprofit organization (12 percent), roughly a quarter who were currently working for a nonprofit organization said they would rather work for government (14 percent) or a private business (13 percent), and almost two-fifths of those currently working for a private company said they would rather work for government (18 percent) or a nonprofit agency (19 percent).

The graduates who expressed a preference to stay in their current sector were hardly uniformly enthusiastic about their imagined future, however. All totaled, roughly a fifth of these "stay-put" graduates said they did not feel strongly about their preference, with the greatest reluctance coming from graduates in the nonprofit sector. While 16 percent of those who went to government and 17 percent of those who went to the private sector said they did not feel strongly about their preferred future, 30 percent of those who went to the nonprofit sector did not feel strongly about their imagined future, perhaps confirming the stress of being in a sector marked by such growth.

The first question in puzzling through these patterns is whether the intention to switch converts to reality. Imagining a career marked by sector switching is one thing, executing it is another. At least for the graduates interviewed for *The New Public Service*, the plans were real. Graduates not only said they were going to move, they mostly did (see figure 2-1).

Figure 2-1. *Career Patterns among Public Policy and Administration Graduates*[a]

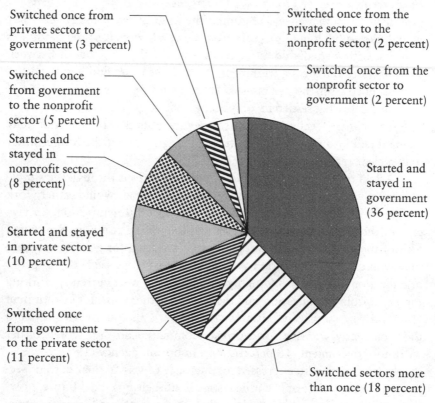

Switched once from private sector to government (3 percent)

Switched once from the private sector to the nonprofit sector (2 percent)

Switched once from government to the nonprofit sector (5 percent)

Switched once from the nonprofit sector to government (2 percent)

Started and stayed in nonprofit sector (8 percent)

Started and stayed in government (36 percent)

Started and stayed in private sector (10 percent)

Switched once from government to the private sector (11 percent)

Switched sectors more than once (18 percent)

N = 1,000
a. Numbers do not add to 100 because of rounding.

The switching rates are not uniform across the three sectors of the new public service, however. Government does not just trail the private and nonprofit sectors in the competition for new graduates; it is also the least likely to hold its talent over time. Regardless of when they went to school, graduates who take their first jobs outside government are more likely to stay put than those who start inside government.

This is not to argue that the private and nonprofit sectors are particularly effective on their own in holding talent. The nonprofit sector was volatile as a first destination, with significant percentages of graduates moving out over time. But when these graduates moved from a private or nonprofit job, they were significantly more likely to move to the other nongovernmental sector than into government. Once outside, they were highly likely to stay outside, in part because government offers so few opportunities for entry at the middle and senior levels.

The second question is whether these data on public policy and administration graduates reflect more general trends affecting the public service. The public service is not the only career marked by increasing motion. Spotty evidence shows that law and business graduates are moving more frequently. According to a tracking study of 10,300 law associates hired between 1988 and 1996, roughly 10 percent had left their private firm within one year, 27 percent within two, 43 percent within three, and 56 percent within four. Although some of the departures likely reflected the natural winnowing that occurs in such a highly competitive field, the anecdotal evidence suggests that associates at the nation's top law firms began cycling out as the allure of compensation wore off and the pressures of making partner took hold.[40]

The graduates' explanations for switching also are instructive. In them, one hears the echoes of conversations that take place in every organization in the global economy. These graduates believe that change is a natural, indeed inevitable, part of one's career. "Nothing is promised to us," said a Harvard graduate. "I have no clue where the next opportunity will come from, or which opportunity will present itself." A 1993 Carnegie Mellon graduate who had started in business and already moved once to a nonprofit offered an even briefer explanation of his intention to switch again: "Life is a long path and there are many forks along the way."

How might the sector switching affect the tides of nonprofit reform? The answer seems clear: as these new public servants move across the sectors, they carry the latest fashions in reform. Like the professionalization of the nonprofit sector, sector switching increases demand for transferable skills, which in turn may increase the portability of specific reform methodologies. In essence, common reform languages facilitate movement across the sectors. Moreover, high levels of sector switching ease the movement of ideas back and forth across now porous boundaries. If a given reform is hot in any one sector, it is likely to be hot in all sectors.

If one word characterizes all of the national trends described above, it is *competition*. Although competition is not new to the sector, the intensity is. As foundations and individuals become more professionalized in their giving, private firms more aggressive in entering what were once pristine nonprofit markets, and talent more selective in the choice of jobs, nonprofit organizations have lost a measure of control over their future. "The potential dilemma for all nonprofit organizations involves their need for resources and the likelihood that the methods used to generate those resources will require sacrifice of control over their use," Weisbrod writes of the commercialization movement. "No source of revenue has unambiguous effects. . . . The conceptual distinction is between revenue that is effectively unconstrained, facilitating advancement of the non-profit's mission, and revenue that is actually constraining, forcing the nonprofit to choose between foregoing the funds or distorting the social mission as its leadership defines it."[41]

He could just as easily have written about the competition for talent or the rise of the Internet. If the sociologists are right, the more nonprofit organizations face the same uncertain environment, the more they will come to look alike.

Local Realities

Even as nationalizing trends create heightened pressure for and interest in nonprofit management reform, local realities alter the probabilities that any single reform idea will sweep the sector. After all, most non-profits operate in limited catchment areas, pay attention to signals from a relatively small number of funders in their sector or localities, and receive their technical assistance from home-grown, locally trained, locally available consultants.

These local ties create enormous barriers to national conversations about management reform, not the least of which is the fragmentation of the knowledge base on what the sector might do to improve organizational effectiveness. As Stone, Bigelow, and Crittenden conclude, localization creates a research agenda of enormous breadth, richness, and complexity as scholars study a handful of organizations at a time, but it provides little opportunity to build connections across studies. "The literature on strategy in nonprofit organizations is considerable," they write. "About 70 relationships have been investigated, and the list of questions is lengthy. However, the research does not present a coherent whole, and the interactions among these various relationships and among components of the strategy process are not clear."[42]

Localization also works against common definitions of what constitutes organizational effectiveness. If, as Robert D. Herman and David O. Renz argue, organizational effectiveness is always a matter of comparison, then localization makes the comparisons especially difficult.[43] One might know what works in Minnesota, but not necessarily whether those lessons apply to Montana or New York.

WHY NONPROFITS SHOULD SEEK LINKAGE. Even as individual organizations might resist national linkages among funders and consultants, they have substantial interest in such efforts. At one level, national linking systems might reduce the volume of reform pressure by forcing reformers to arrange the list of reforms in some reasonable rank order. Better to implement one reform at a time than be asked to implement everything at once. At another level, linking systems might lead reformers to make their disagreements visible before a given initiative takes shape instead of after. Better to reveal the tensions among the four tides of reform before nonprofits have to implement than tally up the lost opportunities and wasted motion after.

That is why nonprofit organizations have some interest in promoting recent efforts to bring funders and consultants together to explore what might be done to improve organizational effectiveness across the sector. To the extent those efforts produce a greater appreciation for the true cost of reform, nonprofits can only benefit.

Nonprofits certainly have reason to applaud creation of Grantmakers for Effective Organizations (GEO). Created in 1997 as an affinity group of the Council on Foundations, GEO has given a growing number of philanthropic foundations the chance to share ideas on how to improve nonprofit performance. With more than three hundred members by 1999, including a broad mix of national and community foundations, GEO has committed itself to promoting dialogue among funders doing work in the field of organizational effectiveness, thereby spreading common sense throughout the ocean of nonprofits. Although GEO endorses an outcomes orientation, it does so under a very broad definition of organizational effectiveness:

There are no easy definitions of organizational effectiveness. It is evidenced by an organization that is able to connect its vision to its goals, its goals to its plans, its plans to its actions, and its actions to results. It is a dynamic, fluctuating, and fluid state, an ever-evolving mosaic of increasing self-awareness and internal development that keeps an organization moving steadily towards its vision. It is about an organization reaping results, not about management for its own sake (a distinction between "efficiency" and "effectiveness"). GEO is committed to the ongoing facets of organizational effectiveness.[44]

GEO is hardly the only counterweight emerging from the national trends, however. A general strengthening has also taken place of the ties that might bind the nonprofit sector as it faces the future, particularly through the use of the Internet. The National Center for Nonprofit Boards joined with the San Francisco-based Support Center for Nonprofit Management in July 1999 to launch Board Cafe, an electronic newsletter that is "short enough to read over a cup of coffee," as part of a general upgrade of its easily accessible website. Three months later, Independent Sector joined with the University of Maryland's Civil Society Initiative to launch NonProfit Pathfinder as a somewhat more static platform for what it called "the definitive online information source for civil society organizations."

Nonprofits also have reason to embrace the Alliance for Nonprofit Management. Created in 1998 through the merger of the Support Centers of America and the Nonprofit Management Association, the Alliance was designed to link technical assistance providers, trainers, and nonprofit associations with a range of national and regional, umbrella, research and academic, publishing, and philanthropic organizations in common pursuit of higher quality across the nonprofit sector. According to Roni Posner, the Alliance's executive director,

> The whole point of Alliance is to create a "big tent" professional association under which many people can work together to "raise the bar"—improve the quality of the management assistance provided to nonprofits. The whole focus is on upgrading the capacity-building provided to nonprofits (not directly to the nonprofits themselves, as they are the clients of our membership). The Alliance is a membership of a huge range of capacity-builders working to reform nonprofit management. Our mission is to provide leadership in civil society by challenging and strengthening those who deliver management and governance support services to nonprofits.

If successful, the Alliance will provide the ties that would bind argu-ably the most important players in the tides of management reform: the consultants who work, design, and implement reforms on behalf of funders and individual organizations. Its greatest asset, which still needs to grow, is a searchable list of technical assistance providers. To the extent the Alliance can get providers to list themselves under its banner, it will have created a unique web that could be used to disseminate promising practices down through the hierarchy of what it calls capacity-builders that currently sort national and local reform ideas into practical implementation.

The Alliance is not dreaming small. It sees itself as the intersection between an extraordinarily broad set of players, inviting the whole group together for the kind of hard-edged conversations about organizational effectiveness, change strategies, and priority setting that are so desperately needed in the field right now. One cannot help but admire the organization for its reach.

Building such an Alliance is not without its challenges, however. For starters, the Alliance does not, cannot, know how many providers there are. No national credentialling system nor any certification or licensing requirements have been established that might yield a broad number against which to measure the depth of the Alliance lists. Experts likely know more about the nation's beauticians and barbers, who continue to be licensed by obscure state agencies, than about the primary providers of training and assistance to the nonprofit sector.

Moreover, the Alliance offers little more than the most basic information about its providers. An organization or consultant can join the Alliance by answering a series of relatively short questions dealing with its size, type of assistance provided, issue areas covered, and specific services offered. Although the Alliance gives providers a chance to state their mission in a subtle endorsement of outcomes measurement, the information produced by a search of the database is best treated as a general introduction to possible providers.

Finally, the Alliance has no capacity to vet the information provided. Although the Alliance does provide members with information to help them "raise the bar on quality" through its *Gold Book of Success Stories* and its electronic newsletter, *PULSE!,* the Alliance cannot vouchsafe for the organizations it lists. To its credit again, the Alliance never advertises the information as anything else.

That is one reason that the GuideStar system is so attractive. It offers what so many advocates, volunteers, individual donors, and philanthropic foundations desire: a way to map the sector as it continues to expand year by year. Tracking the numbers of organizations, employees, and consultants—which the Independent Sector already does on a yearly basis—is no longer enough. Ways must be devised of sorting the sector by more sophisticated measures of performance, impact, quality, and need. For now at least, the only sorters broadly available are to be found on the

Form 990. And that is far from the kind of sophisticated sorting tool the sector appears to require.

None of this is to discount the promise of new organizations such as GEO and the Alliance for providing platforms for more nuanced conversations about the adoption of national reforms. Nor is it to question the continued strengthening of organizations such as the National Center for Nonprofit Boards or the value created by research institutions such as the new Hauser Center for Nonprofit Organizations at Harvard University's John F. Kennedy School of Government and the Aspen Institute's Nonprofit Sector Research Fund.

Nevertheless, the infrastructure of nonprofit management reform is still weak. Many of the sector's most important boundary-spanners are only a year or two old and have yet to be tested by conflict between the competing tides of reform. At least until these efforts reach full maturity, therefore, three local realities suggest that the tides of reform will continue to work with little national discipline. First, states and localities continue to outsource and privatize government functions at a fevered pitch, creating local dependencies that weaken nonprofit attention to national trends. Second, the nonprofit sector is still highly dependent on local networks of consultants and educators to provide the basic training needed to implement management reform. Third, management fashions are still highly responsive to local preferences. To rephrase the old "think globally, act locally" bumper sticker, the nonprofit sector may be thinking nationally about reform, but individual nonprofits continue to behave locally, whether in response to their local funders or because they have no capacity to respond otherwise.

THE FRAGMENTATION OF RESPONSIBILITY. The past twenty years have witnessed the most dramatic, yet least understood, reshaping of the federal government in American administrative history. In the span of just three administrations, from 1984 to 1996, the federal government reduced its total military and civilian work force by a sixth (300,000 jobs), eliminated a quarter of its middle-level management titles (40,000 jobs), and sliced its defense contract work force by nearly a third (1.6 million jobs).

During the same period, however, the federal government's nondefense contract and grant work force grew by a sixth (600,000 jobs), while the senior-most layers of government increased by twenty-two management titles and seven hundred new career and political executives. Remove the Department of Defense and its massive downsizing from the figures, and the true size of the federal work force grew from 5.5 million to 6.3 million, including a dramatic increase in the number of positions created under contracts for services.

Even at the Department of Defense, where the end of the cold war brought an estimated loss of roughly 2.5 million jobs (civilian + uniformed military personnel + contractors + grantees), the service contract work force increased by 100,000 jobs, rising from 2.2 million in 1984 to 2.3 million twelve years later. At nondefense agencies, the increase in service jobs was even more dramatic, rising from 1.3 million to 1.7 million.

Along the way, the bottom of the federal government began to disappear. The year 1997 was the first in civil service history in which the number of middle-level federal employees exceeded the number of lower-level employees. The number of employees in the lower grades of the federal general employment schedule dropped by more than 170,000 between 1993 and 1997, while the number of blue-collar jobs fell an additional 90,000. At the same time, the average employment grade of the lower-level employees who remained in the job increased by its largest margin in a decade, meaning that more jobs were removed at the bottom-most levels than anywhere else. Even as the bottom of government lost nearly 300,000 jobs, the middle of government grew slightly. Notwithstanding the loss of 40,000 middle-management jobs and the separation of thousands of about-to-retire employees, the average middle-level pay grade increased.

Once again, the key question is how the downsizing might affect the tides of nonprofit reform. The first answer is that many of the jobs outsourced by the federal government may have ended up in state and local government, private firms, and nonprofit agencies. The problem is that no one knows for sure. Some of the bottom-level jobs disappeared forever; others likely ended up in service contracts. Lacking careful tracking data, one can only have suspicions about where the jobs finally went. For example, many of the jobs lost during the downsizing could have been obsolete, but the federal government did not have the means to eliminate them until the early 1990s. Those jobs may not have suddenly become obsolete, but they most certainly became immediately expendable.

The second answer is that the outsourcing fever is spreading rapidly from Washington, D.C., downward to state and local government, where private firms are competing for a growing share of public work in managing everything from prisons (Corrections Corporation of America) to welfare (Lockheed Martin IMS). As Ryan argues, "The real news is not the appearance of a few high-profile for-profit players on the field but rather the underlying changes that have made their entry and rapid growth possible. While many nonprofits are still reeling from cutbacks on social spending, for-profits are celebrating the fact that government outsourcing is still growing in so many areas."[45]

The politics of outsourcing suggests that the flow will not soon abate. It is the easiest way to keep government looking small and is the reform that satisfies nearly every institution involved. At the federal level, for example, presidents support outsourcing because it gives them the right to claim that they, not Congress, control the instruments of government; Congress, because members are so dependent on contractors for financial support; Democrats, because a smaller government headcount provides a defense against their image as the party of tax and spend; Republicans, because it strengthens their base of business support; and contractors, because they are contractors. Even civil servants have incentives to favor a small civil service, whether because it may increase public confidence or because it increases their annual performance appraisals. Having a government that looks smaller but delivers at least as much also appears to increase incumbency advantages, whether that incumbent happens to be a Democrat or Republican, president or mayor. Keeping government looking small is the work force policy that satisfies almost every political preference. By cutting the federal headcount even as the program agenda remains steady or expands, the federal government gives the public what it wants: the savings implied in downsizing with the benefits of an activist program agenda. It is also one way for America's elected and appointed leaders to claim progress in cutting costs, while reaping significant political benefits.

Outsourcing may be a national fever that has spread downward to the states and localities, but it is anything but national in its impact. At least in welfare reform, outsourcing is being implemented at random, which means that the outsourcing fever affects nonprofits in different ways depending on where they are located. California is implementing its state and county outsourcing in different ways from Texas; Florida is implementing it in different ways from Michigan and Milwaukee. Although everyone seems to want some form of performance contracting, no agreement exists on what those contracts should specify. At the same time, little evidence is available that states or localities are learning from each other as they push jobs and responsibilities outward. Despite good evidence that contracting out will affect how nonprofits deliver services, little systematic information has been gathered on what might be happening

---

Box 2-1. Courses Offered by the Maryland Association of Nonprofits

November 3
  Preparing the 990
  Nonprofit Finances for Board
    Members
November 4
  Special Accounting Considerations
  Proposal Writing Specifics
November 9
  Strategically Planning Success
November 10
  Planning for Effective Fundraising
November 11
  Managing the New Accounting,
    Auditing & Tax Environment

November 16
  Evaluation: Measuring Your
    Success
November 17
  Budgeting Basics
  Redefining Success: Integrating
    Professional
  Achievement with Life's Other
    Demands
November 18
  Standards for Excellence

---

to the sector as outsourcing grows.[46] The result is toxic: little cross-jurisdictional information, intense pressure to outsource, limited resources for research, and endless forms of implementation. It is just the kind of setting where the tides of reform can do their greatest damage.

THE FRAGMENTATION OF LEARNING. Even a cursory review of the training programs currently offered by local support centers and nonprofit associations suggests the lack of any agreement on reform. Consider the courses offered in November 1999 by the Maryland Association of Nonprofits, which is one of the most professionally run of the statewide organizations serving nonprofits on the East Coast (see box 2-1).

The list is hardly different from the calendars of dozens of other training organizations. Consider the extensive list offered by the San Francisco Support Center, which sets a parallel standard of excellence among the organizations one finds on the West Coast (see box 2-2).

Without generalizing beyond the limits of reason, the two lists offer important hints about the state of nonprofit management training. First, the lists contain a relatively large number of courses that would be either offered in-house at most of America's larger private corporations or purchased from outside contractors. Although one cannot assess sector capacity by merely reading down a list of courses, there is some evidence here that nonprofits in Maryland and San Francisco may need management basics more than they need management reform. *Reengineering an*

Box 2-2. *Courses offered by the San Francisco Support Center*

November 1
  Beat the Clock! Effectively
    Managing Your Time
  Intermediate Word 97 for Windows
November 2
  Getting Started in Planned Giving
  Introduction to Access 97 for
    Windows
  Introduction to PageMaker 6.5 for
    the Mac
November 5
  Coaching Intensive for Executive
    Directors: Your Personal Power
    Can Make the Difference
  Hiring a Technology Consultant
  Introduction to FileMaker Pro 4.0
November 9
  Introduction to Excel 97 for
    Windows
  Creative Ways to Crack the Media:
    Enhancing Your Institution's
    Viability and Mission
November 10
  Supervision: Helping People Achieve
    Results
  Intermediate PageMaker 6.5 for
    Windows
  Intermediate Web Page Production
    and HTML
November 15
  Effective Communication & Conflict
    Resolution Skills
  Introduction to Access 97 for
    Windows

November 16
  Database Camp for Access 97
  Designing and Implementing a
    Community Needs Assessment
  Introduction to Web Page
    Production and HTML
November 17
  Introduction to Investing
  Introduction to Word 97 for
    Windows
  Intermediate FileMaker Pro
November 18
  Demonstration: Blackbaud
    Accounting Software for
    Nonprofits
  Intermediate Access 97 for Windows
  Intermediate Excel 98 for the Mac
November 19
  Beyond Basic Bookkeeping: Applying
    Skills to the Nonprofit
    Environment
  Intermediate Word 98 for the Mac
  Networking Basics for Non-Techies
November 22
  Intermediate Excel 97 for Windows
November 23
  Database Camp for Access 97
November 30
  Writing Successful Grant Proposals:
    A Two-Day Workshop
  Database Camp for Access 97
  Introduction to FileMaker Pro 4.0

---

organization is difficult if it has not been engineered in the first place. Second, the lists suggest that there is more demand for help in managing stress, time, and money than in launching reform agendas. To the extent the lists reflect the market for training, they suggest that the nonprofit sector is enduring the best and worst of times. Courses on managing money and technology stand side by side with courses on managing one's own life and career.

THE FRAGMENTATION OF ASSISTANCE. Even if training curricula were standardized across the country, most nonprofits and their funders still rely on local sources of technical assistance to help implement manage-ment reform. And those local sources are anything but unified on which reforms to pursue.

The local differences are easy to spot in the Maryland and San Fran-cisco training programs. Again assuming that the training programs reveal the market for information, the two sites have different training needs, in part because they have different nonprofit cultures. The San Francisco Support Center does not offer coursework on standards, for ex-ample, because the standards movement has not taken root in Northern California. Meanwhile, the Maryland Association of Nonprofits does not offer much coursework on technology because the mid-Atlantic commu-nity it serves is either ahead in the area or much further behind. Funder preferences explain at least some of the difference. Maryland funders care deeply about technology, for example. However, they have chosen differ-ent methods for promoting change, not the least of which is the circuit rider model that the Eugene and Agnes Meyer Foundation has adopted for its District of Columbia grantees.[47]

A substantial explanation for the differences involves local history, culture, educational resources, and technical assistance, all of which reflect local traditions. As the survey of nonprofit management associa-tions will suggest, some states have embraced standards reform, while others have drifted more toward outcomes management; some have become entranced by reengineering, while others have warmed to trans-parency. The variation may reflect corporate traditions; for example, leading Atlantans toward a stronger embrace of entrepreneurism and Minnesotans toward technology, Californians to liberation management and Texans to war on waste. It may also be rooted in local politics, out-sourcing pressures, and whatever scandal may have reached the papers. And it most certainly reflects what local funders think should be done to strengthen nonprofit capacity. Although GEO represents a significant effort to open a national dialogue about effectiveness, most of the con-versation to date has been made at the local level in the form of regional associations of grantmakers.[48]

There are ways to provide national expertise to local organizations, including the kinds of network imagined by the Alliance for Nonprofit Management. There is also growing interest in the nonprofit sector as a national consulting market. In 1999, for example, Bain & Company, a global strategy consulting firm, launched the Bridge Group to provide consulting services to nonprofits. Led by former Bain principal Jeffrey Bradach, funded in part by philanthropic foundations, and staffed primarily by its socially conscious younger staff, the Bridge Group promises to "take the best of the strategy consulting capabilities of the for-profit sector and customize and apply them to the challenges facing nonprofit managers." Adopting what it labels as a single measure of success in "the extent to which its consulting and knowledge dissemination activities provide nonprofit organizations with breakthrough results in performance," the Bridge Group imagines a relatively small practice based on consulting relationships with "high potential nonprofits" and foundation-funded studies that "aimed at systematically distilling and disseminating the experience and knowledge developed through consulting for the benefit of other nonprofit managers and sector participants."

Whether Bain's culture, which is built around its mission to "help our clients create such high levels of economic value that together we set new standards of excellence in our respective industries," and its general definition of organizational effectiveness as a strategic management question will translate into nonprofit credibility is yet to be seen. No matter how well fenced by a nonprofit ethos, and no matter how well motivated to provide nonprofit-relevant consulting, the Bridge Group is still a branch of Bain & Company. If successful, the effort could provoke other for-profit firms to enter the business, accomplishing in one stroke what the Alliance for Nonprofit Management has been struggling to accomplish one local provider at a time. But given its core mission as a private consulting firm, the Bain effort will likely concentrate on nationally visible nonprofits such as the Red Cross, leaving most nonprofits to continue purchasing their technical assistance from local providers. To the extent local nonprofits can turn to research-driven assistance from operating foundations such as the Amherst Wilder Foundation in St. Paul, Minnesota, that advice is likely to feature national links. But to the extent they must rely on their own resources to purchase support, they must do the best they can with the available capacity.

Even as one can applaud the decision of high-end private consulting firms such as Bain & Company, McKinsey, and the Boston Consulting Group to provide pro bono or low-cost services to nonprofits, even as one can find occasional examples of for-profit firms such as the Conservation Company, Community Wealth Ventures, and Kubler Wirka that specialize in the nonprofit sector, and even as one can celebrate national foundations such as the David and Lucile Packard Foundation and the Pew Charitable Trusts and regional foundations such as the McKnight Foundation and Meyer Foundation for providing the dollars to purchase technical assistance, the reality is that most small- to medium-sized non-profits rely on local capacity. There is no national market for consulting services, and rarely much of a local market. Despite the availability of some local search engines (see the San Francisco Support Center and Maryland Association of Nonprofit Organization websites), most non-profits depend on personal networks, board members, and funders to make the choice of consultants.

A second strategy is to build local sources of educational training that are linked nationally. Toward that model, in 1998 the W. K. Kellogg Foundation made $12.5 million in grants to eighteen regional partnerships to build comprehensive education programs for nonprofit and public leaders. The grants were designed around the belief that nonprofit leaders need new management skills, particularly in policy and financial development, and that regional programs could act as more authentic magnets than nationally rooted programs.

The programs themselves are remarkably diverse, from educating entry-level human service professionals at American Humanics in Kansas City, to exposing nonprofit leaders to different cultures at the City University of New York, creating distance learning opportunities through a collaboration involving Society for Nonprofit Organizations, University of Wisconsin Extension Service, and Murphy Communications Inc., finding new minority leaders through another collaboration among High Point University, North Carolina Central University, and Shaw University, and addressing the needs of faith-based enterprises at the Yale Divinity School. Once beyond the broad national goal of improving management, and once past the grants to national programs at Harvard and Case Western Reserve, however, it is not clear that the Kellogg program will have a nationalizing effect, nor was it intended to do so.

Despite these differences, a given locality can bend a given reform to its own history and culture in only so many ways. Take the standards movement as an example. Although Minnesota and Maryland have very different histories and culture, both state associations of nonprofits have virtually identical standards for excellence. The reasons are simple. When Minnesota began its standards-setting process, it turned to the Maryland Association of Nonprofit Organizations for help. Minnesota acknowledges its debt of gratitude in its introduction of standards. Nevertheless, even here, the two codes are not identical. Minnesota puts heavier emphasis on mission than Maryland and has greater emphasis on technology, while Maryland puts more emphasis on legal issues and conflict of interest. Compared side by side, history and culture work their will. Minnesota writes of "mission and values," while Maryland talks of "mission and program"; Minnesota talks of "information and technology," while Maryland addresses "openness"; Minnesota features "partnership and alliances," while Maryland puts the topic under "public affairs and public policy." The differences reflect history and culture. Even if leaders of the two efforts, Jon Pratt of Minnesota and Peter Berns of Maryland, had been twins raised apart, the two sets of standards would have been different, if only because of the local cultures. Ultimately, even as a given tide constrains local flexibility, it must conform to the terrain, even as it remakes it.

One last point is in order before turning to the tides of reform in more detail. Despite the growing inventory of nonprofit graduate programs, there is little evidence that students are learning the kind of skills that would constitute a barrier against the tides of reform. To the contrary, many of the graduates interviewed for *The New Public Service* reported significant gaps in their training. Asked, for example, to list the skills that they viewed as very important to their career success, the one thousand graduates listed at the top maintaining ethical standards, leading others, managing conflict, managing information technology, and managing innovation and change. Significant agreement was evident across the sectors (see table 2-2). Nevertheless, graduates who were working in the nonprofit sector at the time of the interviews put raising money much higher on their list of concerns (51 percent rated it a very important skill) than graduates in government (17 percent of federal government employees rated it a very important skill) or the private sector (34 percent).

When asked how well their graduate programs did in delivering those skills, the graduates were less than enthusiastic about their learning. Whereas 82 percent said maintaining ethical standards was very important to their career success, only 48 percent said their graduate school had been very helpful teaching the skill; whereas 72 percent said leading others was very important, only 42 said their graduate school had been very helpful teaching that skill. The gaps continue down the list. The gap on managing conflict was 34 percent; managing information technology, 29 percent; managing change, 22 percent; and raising revenue, 15 percent. The only skill that graduates said their schools had been too helpful in teaching

Table 2-2. *The Skills Needed for Success*

Percent who said skill was very important for job success

Skill	Government			Private sector (N = 275)	Non-profit (N = 166)
	Federal (N = 117)	State (N = 167)	Local (N = 109)		
Maintaining ethical standards	81	75	84	81	89
Leading others	70	62	75	75	76
Managing conflict	52	54	67	64	66
Managing information and communication technology	57	54	67	64	66
Influencing policymakers	56	54	55	57	54
Managing innovation and change	52	53	55	57	57
Doing policy analysis	64	69	61	41	55
Budgeting and public finance	56	54	64	45	46
Managing a diverse work force	50	39	43	40	42
Analyzing and influencing public opinion	36	34	35	35	42
Raising money and generating extra revenue	17	21	19	34	51
Managing media relations	25	23	29	27	31
Writing regulations and legislation	37	35	23	22	22

involved policy analysis: 65 percent said their schools had been very helpful, but only 55 percent identified the skill as very important.

The gaps suggest that the nation's top graduate programs may be doing well educating the next generation of nonprofit leaders as policy analysts, but that they may be failing in giving them the skills to sort among competing ideas for reform. Facing increased pressure to do something, anything, to strengthen their organizations' management, these graduates may not have the skills to say no. That can only increase the damage that the tides can do.

CHAPTER THREE

The Tides of Reform

The choice of tides as a metaphor for describing nonprofit reform leads inevitably to images of periodicity and motion. Like the tides of the ocean, the tides of reform will never cease. Even if the current pressure for reform were to suddenly calm, the tides would rise and fall regardless, bringing their periodic shifts in ideology to the nonprofit sector just as they have to government and private firms for hundreds of years. And like the tides of the ocean, the tides of reform carry a vast collection of treasure and waste, some of which gets used by nonprofits, some of which gets tossed back into the ocean in due course.

The decision about what gets defined as treasure and waste depends in part on who sponsors a given reform. In government, for example, the tides of reform are pulled across organizations by the separation of powers and constitutional prerogatives. Congress has long been the source of war on waste and watchful eye, pressing to open government to the sunshine as part of its enduring effort to control administrative discretion, while the presidency has been the sponsor of both scientific and liberation management in the continuing attempt to wrest that administrative discretion from Congress. Ever was it thus that the two branches pull government in and out of the sunshine, back and forth through wars on waste, and through countless organizations, reorganizations, reinventings, and reengineerings.

It is not clear just who exerts control over the nonprofit tides. At one level, Congress and the president act as the counterpulls, if only because their embrace of reform influences the independent sector through out-sourcing, accounting standards, and prevailing images of best practice. Hence, the rise of performance management in the federal government has clearly accelerated its embrace by nonprofit funders, in part because the Government Performance and Results Act encourages the use of out-comes for contracting. At a second level, national and community funders compete for control, if only because national funders are so powerful in shaping the broad winds of change, while community funders and local corporations tend to represent local interests and clients. Sometimes the national and community funders are the same, as with the Lilly Endow-ment in Indianapolis and the Pew Charitable Trusts in Philadelphia. When the national and local are in alignment, as in Philadelphia, they can create a powerful pull for reform. But when they are in conflict, they can confuse more than improve, forcing local organizations to choose which funder to satisfy.

At still another level, clients and the media act as counterpulls, one dri-ving efforts to improve responsiveness and sensitivity, the other fueling the scandals that undergird wars on waste and inefficiency. Even as clients want familiarity and individualized service, the war on waste demands economy at any cost, even if it undermines the personalized relationships that many nonprofits believe distinguish their organizations from private firms.

Unfortunately, the nonprofit sector is caught in the middle of an unre-lenting contest between competing philosophies and advocates of reform, all of which produce significant motion back and forth across different reform ideologies. Lacking the kind of linking systems described in chap-ter 2, the only way to survive in such a system is to recognize the tides when they come ashore, harvest the good ideas that they might contain, and let them wash back out to sea with minimal damage. Simply stated, the organization must protect itself against adopting any single reform, lest it find itself forced to change course when the next reform wave arrives.

The problem is that the nonprofit sector has yet to develop the knowl-edge base to help individual organizations choose the reform approach that benefits them the most. The sector has yet to reach an agreement on any outcome measure at all for reform. It is as if reform is somehow exempt from the very kinds of tests that reformers expect nonprofits to demand of their own work. For example, advocates of outcomes mea-surement should provide some metric against which to evaluate the rela-tive benefit of their preferred reform. Is outcomes measurement a more useful tool than, say, a standards model? Does it yield a better cost-benefit ratio than a strategic alliance or posting an organization's Form 990 on the Internet? Just what is the expected gain in productivity or impact from implementing the United Way of America's outcomes measurement system?

Unfortunately, measuring the effectiveness of efforts to improve organizational effectiveness is impossible without some clearly understood definition of what effectiveness is. Given the current state of the field of nonprofit studies, that definition is still well beyond reach. Daniel P. Forbes is so discouraged by the lack of systematic research that he titled his 1998 literature review "Measuring the Unmeasurable," while Herman and Renz argue that most academic researchers are simply "uninterested in effectiveness."[49] Absent rigorous measures against which to assess effectiveness, and despite some progress in operationalizing the concept of public value, scholars and practitioners might assume that nonprofit effectiveness is essentially the same as business effectiveness. Government has done the same thing for years. Furthermore, reformers usually make their case more on theological than empirical grounds. What choice do they have?

Scientific Management

Scientific management is arguably the oldest of the reform tides regardless of sector. The tide is rooted in the long-standing belief that certain organizational practices constitute essentials of good management and can be tracked back in time to the organization of heavy industry and armies. The power of scientific management lies in its profound surety that inviolable principles can be expressed as absolutes for success. It is a tide dominated by words such as *should* and *must*, and it tends to arise in the form of checklists, templates, and benchmarks that tell a given organization exactly how to do its work. It is as close as the sector gets to Frederick Taylor's one best way. Box 3-1 summarizes the key characteristics of the tide.

Scientific management uses a compliance model of accountability, which is one of three general approaches to monitoring organizational improvement. Unlike capacity-based accountability, which puts its faith in providing the tools (be they human, technological, or motivational) needed for improvement, or performance-based accountability, which puts its emphasis on setting goals (whether measurable or not) that pull

---

Box 3-1. *Characteristics of Scientific Management*

Common expression: Standards, codes of conduct

Central assumption: A set of core practices makes all organizations effective

Focus: Internal improvement

Primary implementor: Individual organizations

Accountability model: Compliance

Cost of implementation: High

Time to higher performance: Moderate to long, particularly if new systems are involved

Measurability of change: High

Level of independence: Low

Stress on organization: High

Patron saint: Frederick Taylor

Patron organization: National Charities Information Bureau

Strengths: Promotion of basic good practices

Weaknesses: Possible focus on unimportant elements of organizational performance

---

the organization toward a hoped-for future, compliance-based accountability is built around the idea that organizational improvement flows from a set of precise rules for conduct.[50] The choice of one model does not necessarily exclude the others. The United Way of America's outcomes initiative is firmly rooted in a performance-based model of accountabililty, for example, but is expressed to individual nonprofits in compliance terms; that is, clear rules and languages govern the implementation of the United Way's focusing on outcomes initiative.

Nevertheless, the three models envision different points of intervention, mechanisms, and roles for organizational leaders in improving accountability. Compliance accountability tends to be used after an implementation activity to reveal faithful execution, or the lack thereof, while performance accountability is used before the implementation activity to set broad goals. Perhaps most important are the primary mechanism for achieving change:

The common currency of compliance accountability is rules and regulations, whether dealing with procurement, travel, personnel, or a specific policy. The rules are reinforced through cumbersome signature and approval systems. In contrast, performance account-ability emerged from the establishment of incentives, the most familiar of which are the pay for performance systems [embedded in most personnel systems]. Capacity building focuses on technologies, broadly defined to include human capital and the tools of manage-ment. In addition, capacity building includes both program and organizational redesign; that is, the development of workable pro-grams and responsive structures.[51]

Because of its highly decentralized structure and its many subsectors, the nonprofit sector has mostly avoided the tight compliance systems that provoked Gore's reinventing government campaign. Rarely does one encounter the kind of us-against-them rhetoric in the nonprofit literature that dominated the vice president's first reinventing government report: "From the 1930s through the 1960s, we built large, top-down, centralized bureaucracies to do the public's business. They were patterned after the corporate structures of the age: hierarchical bureaucracies in which tasks were broken into simple parts, each the responsibility of a different layer of employees, each defined by specific rules and regulations. With their rigid preoccupation with standard operating procedure, their vertical chains of command, and their standardized services, these bureaucracies were steady—but slow and cumbersome."[52] This is why the sector should be careful about embracing deep compliance-based models of accountability. Long after the reforms have passed, the rules they create will remain.

This is not to argue that nonprofit organizations cannot get better, nor that funders have no business setting basic minimums for financial man-agement, board governance, conflict of interest, public advocacy, and so forth. After all, the nonprofit sector does not exist outside the reach of contracting, tax, and labor law. Good financial reporting is essential for more than just stewardship. It is also a staple of an innovating organiza-tion. Organizations cannot make the leaps of faith inherent in new ideas if they do not know the limits of their financial endurance and funder support.[53] At the same time, the nonprofit sector and its funders would do well to worry about the lasting effects of recommending new manage-ment systems and organizational units. If the federal government is a guide, those systems and units are likely to stay for a very long time.

Scientific management is built around the basic notion that all well-performing organizations have certain common characteristics. That is certainly the central theme of the standards for excellence and codes of conduct that has emerged in the nonprofit sector over the past decade, whether through organizations such as the National Charities Information Bureau or the International Committee on Fundraising Organizations (ICFO), which joined the standards movement in 1999 by issuing uniform standards that grantmakers can use to assure proper management and internal controls. Designed to reduce the "chances of incompetence or fraud," therefore using a familiar war on waste rhetoric to support uniformity, the ICFO standards can be taken as a minimum benchmark against which to measure the more stringent standards being issued in Canada, the United Kingdom, and the United States.

The degree to which competing sets of standards are loose or tight depends in large measure upon who is doing the standard setting. Compare as examples the standards issued by the national Council of Better Business Bureaus' Philanthropic Advisory Service in 1999 (hereafter referred to as the Better Business Bureau standards) and the Maryland Association of Nonprofit Organizations in 1998. The Better Business Bureau standards could not be more precise. "Soliciting organizations" are to apply "a reasonable percentage of total income from all sources (at least 50 percent) . . . to the programs and activities directly related to the purposes for which the organization exists," hold fundraising costs to a reasonable minimum "not exceeding 35 percent of related contributions," and "shall substantiate on request" the link between the funds requested and "the programs and activities described in solicitations."[54]

(Readers who need another reminder about local variation could also compare the Better Business Bureau standards with the seven benchmarks for excellence promulgated in 1999 by the Fund for the City of New York, a private operating foundation established by the Ford Foundation in 1968. Although the Fund's new standards track closely with Maryland's and Minnesota's, they are considerably less prescriptive in tone. On fund-raising, for example, the Fund's benchmarks are mostly broad suggestions toward "collaboration among the executive, finance, program, and development departments in all phases of the fund development process, from planning to implementing funding strategies" or the adoption of "a fund development plan" that "reflects the agency's mission, goals, and objectives.")[55]

Although the Maryland standards are prescriptive, they tend to avoid the specific thresholds embedded in the Better Business effort. According to the association's fund-raising standard, for example, "A nonprofit's fundraising costs should be reasonable over time. On average, over a five year period, a nonprofit should realize charitable contributions from fundraising activities that are at least three times the amount spent on fundraising. Organizations whose fundraising ratio is less than 3:1 should demonstrate progress that they are making steady progress toward achieving this goal, or should be able to justify why a 3:1 ratio is not appropriate for the individual organization."[56]

The two sets of standards also rely on different enforcement mechanisms. The Better Business Bureau standards were designed to be enforced by donors such as the United Way of the Greater Dayton Area, which adopted the standards in early 1999. At least as the lead paragraphs of the *Chronicle of Philanthropy* story on the adoption suggest, the standards were to be used to discipline poor performers: "Each year, the Children's Medical Center in Dayton, Ohio, receives $50,000 or more in donations from the local United Ways. But this year, the pediatric hospital won't receive a penny unless it convinces the local Better Business Bureau that the institution meets all 16 of the bureau's standards for charity fundraising and governance. And the Children's Medical Center is not the only non-profit organization facing that requirement."[57]

The Better Business Bureau standards were developed outside the nonprofit sector, while the Maryland standards were developed by a working group of association members to be promoted to nonprofits by nonprofits. The Maryland document contains no language about fraud, waste, and abuse, nor any references to the need to prevent incompetence. The Maryland standards rely on the nonprofit sector's desire to increase public confidence: "Based on fundamental values—such as honesty, integrity, fairness, respect, responsibility, and accountability—these Standards describe how nonprofits should act to be ethical and be accountable in their program operations, human resources, financial management and fundraising." Built around eight guiding principles (for example, "An organization's fundraising program should be maintained on a foundation of truthfulness and responsible stewardship") and fifty-five specific standards, Maryland's effort is of the community and for the community but clearly recognizes the crisis of legitimacy.[58] The emphasis is on moral suasion, not external inspection.

This is not to suggest that the Maryland standards have no bite. If successful, the standards will become part of a broad self-study and peer-review certification process that will set successful nonprofits apart from

the rest of their competitors. Merely entering the process signals an organization's commitment to improvement, if only because the self-study
itself involves several hundred hours of work and a $250 fee for mem-
bers. The application packet starts with a Certification Statement to be
signed by the board chair as well as the chief professional officer and pro-
ceeds through an eight-page request for a variety of information in both
questionnaire and documentary form. To be certified as having met the
Standards of Excellence, and thereby eligible to use the Standards of
Excellence logo for a period not to exceed three years, an organization
must present its written mission statement (Standard IA1) and provide
the date on which the board of directors most recently reviewed the statement; supply copies of all board minutes from the last twelve months
(Standard IIC5) and report on all delegated decisionmaking authority
given to a committee in any specific subject areas; list current board members with specific information on principal employer, occupation, and
term, as well as explanations for any relationships "by blood or mar-
riage" between board members and staff; describe the organization's
method for employee performance evaluation and orientation program
(Standard IVC1); provide the four most recent internal financial statements and reports, and a description of procedures for receiving confidential reports of known or suspected financial improprieties by employees (Standard VA5).[59] Maryland may allow some wiggle room in
encouraging nonprofits to improve, but its standards are much deeper
and more rigorous than the guidelines used by the Better Business
Bureaus.

The strength of such efforts is obvious: the nonprofit sector cannot
doubt what is expected by way of improvement. Not only are most of the
standards measurable, but progress also is easily assessed. An organization either has a performance appraisal process or it does not; its board
either meets three times (Better Business Bureau) or six times (Maryland)
a year or it does not. The weakness is that the recommendations reach
well beyond the knowledge base on organizational effectiveness.

The best available research suggests, for example, that board engage-
ment may not be the place to start building an effective organization.
Although some limited evidence does suggest that more effective boards
result in more effective organizations, it is not always clear just what the
causal relationship is. Effective organizations could recruit effective
boards, not vice versa. "Whether more effective boards do more, do different things, or do what they do better (or some combination) than less

effective boards is not clear," write Herman and Renz of the existing literature. "Effective managers and staff might improve organizational effectiveness and, thus, be more effective at recruiting better board members, resulting in more effective boards."[60]

Nevertheless, the march of standards continues, in part because standards provide one way to measure nonprofits against each other, in part because many nonprofits have so far to go in developing the basic systems they need for minimal accountability and effectiveness. Much as one can complain about the overapplication of standards, there is no doubt that the standards movement provides at least some help to organizations that want to see where the average nonprofit should be on simple indicators such as board activities.

The question is how far to push standards, not just as an informational resource, but as a tool for sorting effective nonprofits from ineffective. With so many nonprofits competing for the same dollars, one can hardly blame foundations for using standards as one indicator in selecting grantees. But whether they should use standards in making final funding decisions is an entirely different question. Imagine, for a moment, the difficulties in actually using standards to generate a summative measure of organizational effectiveness. Even if one could develop hard measures of finance, mission, record keeping, and operations, foundations would be hard pressed to demonstrate a link between any single measure and overall organizational effectiveness. There is no evidence, for example, that having a merit pay system for staff is related to organizational effectiveness, or that holding six board meetings instead of three improves performance, or that adopting a strategic planning process is somehow going to improve outcomes.[61]

Although those invloved in the effort foreswear any commitment to a given school of management, such efforts are, in fact, nearly perfect examples of scientific management. Whatever the measurement effort might include by way of individual items, it assumes that an organization that scores higher on a given inventory of measures is somehow more effective than one that scores lower, which is a classic expression of scientific management. By intent or accident, the organization that scores 100 out of 100 would, in fact, be perfect. One can almost see Frederick Taylor, with his stopwatch and clipboard, at work.

The problem is the use of such systems to make decisions and create incentives for organizational reform. Scientific management may say that there is one best way, but decades of study suggest that there may be many true ways and little solid ground exists on which to recommend one way over another. Should organizations start with the board or the staff? Should they build better financial management systems or fund-raising units? Should they give their executives better benefits or increase front-line salaries? In a perfect world, there would be no need to choose. Organizations would have the resources to do it all simultaneously. But the nonprofit sector is not a perfect world.

War on Waste

Like scientific management, the war on waste is driven by a belief that there is a "right" number of people and organizations for doing a specific nonprofit job. What makes the war on waste different from scientific management is its general belief that the right number of people and organizations is always less. Built around Taylor's vision of the one best way, the war on waste is motivated by the desire for cost savings, whether through downsizing, mergers, or the outright "obliteration," as Michael Hammer called it, of obsolete organizations. It is also motivated by the desire to eliminate fraud, waste, and incompetence inside organizations by imposing strict controls on financial discretion. (See box 3-2 for the key characteristics of war on waste.)

Also unlike scientific management, the war on waste tends to view employees and organizations as primarily interested in their own survival, even if that survival is to the detriment of competitiveness, performance, or broad social goals. And while scientific management puts its faith on the organization itself to implement reform, the war on waste seeks its impact mostly from the outside through reengineering, reorganizations, mergers, alliances, acquisitions, and broad downsizings.

From a historical perspective, the war on waste received its greatest boost during the welfare fraud hearings of the 1970s. Having discovered billions in fraud at the Department of Health, Education, and Welfare, Congress created the first federal inspector general (IG) in 1976 to act as a quasi-independent watchdog over wasteful federal bureaucrats. By 1998, the concept had been expanded to cover fifty-seven departments and agencies—thirty entities headed by agency-appointed IGs and twenty-seven headed by presidentially appointed and Senate-confirmed IGs.

The basic thrust of the IG concept was remarkably simple. At one level, it merely consolidated what were then dozens of separate, often

---

Box 3-2. *Characteristics of War on Waste*

Common expressions: Reorganization, downsizing, strategic alliances, reengineering

Central assumption: Staff, processes, and subsectors can be organized to create maximum efficiency

Focus: External efficiency

Primary implementor: Large funders or collections of nonprofits

Accountability model: Compliance and/or performance

Cost of implementation: High

Time to higher performance: Short to long depending on degree of reorganization

Measurability of change: High

Level of independence: Low to high

Stress on organization: High

Patron saint: Michael Hammer

Patron organizations: Local corporations and funders

Strengths: Elimination of duplication, concentration of funding resources

Weaknesses: Reductions in diversity, organization fear

---

scattered, audit and investigation units into single operations headed by a presidential appointee. In giving new impetus to the search for accountability, the act envisioned greater resources for the IGs, a hope expressed throughout the legislative process. Thus, as the number of Offices of Inspector General (OIGs) continued to grow, so, too, did the staff and resources. Despite staff cuts across the nondefense agencies of government, the OIGs grew by almost 25 percent over the 1980s.

At a second level, however, the IG represented a major investment in monitoring government. The IGs were not just any officers of government. They were responsible for ferreting out wrongdoing by creating the odium of deterrence, which can only be translated into the word *fear*. Working from clearly defined financial standards and with broad powers to issue subpoenas and open confidential investigations, the IGs earned a well-deserved reputation for "gotcha" behavior. Because they assessed their own performance more by the number of cases opened than by any credible measure of fraud prevented, their greatest success was in driving fear into the federal government, which prompted a stinging rebuke early in Gore's reinventing government report. "The standard by which they are evaluated is finding error or fraud," the report argued. "The more frequently they find mistakes, the more successful they are judged to be. As a result, the IG staffs often develop adversarial relations with agency managers—who, in trying to do things better, may break rules."[62]

The nonprofit sector has not been immune from this kind of single-minded focus on finding fault, if only because nonprofits are part of the vast set of organizations that the IGs are free to audit and investigate. Any organization that accepts a single dollar of federal funding can find itself at the receiving end of an IG review. More important, as evidenced by the rhetoric surrounding the launch of the Better Business Bureau standards, the nonprofit sector has been sucked into the same conversation about inefficiency, waste, and duplication that led to the rise of the IG concept in the first place. That conversation may have taken somewhat different forms, but it is eerily familiar to the fraud-busting rhetoric in Washington and state capitols nonetheless.

That conversation has produced a mix of reform recommendations across the sector, some driven by a performance-based model about how strategic partnerships, alliances, and collaborations; others driven by a compliance-based presumption of waste until proven efficient. Despite its angry title, which comes out of the tides of government reform, the war on waste philosophy can be tied to a forward-looking, performance-based model as a device for preventing needless waste and inefficiency, largely through careful organizational design.

On the performance accountability side, consider two examples of how the war on waste might work to strengthen performance. The first involves the rising prominence of strategic alliance as a model of nonprofit collaboration. Although nonprofits have been collaborating in one form or another since Alexis de Tocqueville celebrated America's penchant for associations in the 1830s, strategic alliances emerged as a concept in the mid-1980s in a *Harvard Business Review* article—by Joanne Scheff and marketing guru Philip Kotler—on how the arts can survive in lean times. Unlike the Ford Foundation and Pew Charitable Trusts, which both launched new funding programs in 1999 to expand public support for the arts, Scheff and Kotler take the financial condition of the subsector as a given and offer strategic alliances as the answer. Instead of trying to alter demand or funding, they argue for consolidating supply. (The Ford and Pew initiatives are perfect examples of how the philanthropic community can alter performance through external capacity building.)

Consider how Scheff and Kotler structure their call for alliances with a business-oriented forecast of a dire future:

> The arts have been hard hit by shrinking audiences and rising debt. Cuts in government funding have become severe, and many sources of funding—especially government agencies and private foundations—have been earmarking grants for specific programs so that less is available for general operating budgets. Corporate, foundation, and business support is often provided on the condition that arts organizations become leaner, more business oriented, and supportive of the donor's marketing objectives. Whereas the business sector has realized considerable gains in productivity throughout most of [the twentieth] century as well as benefits from cost cutting and downsizing, a performance of Beethoven's Fifth Symphony will always require about 36 minutes and an orchestra of 70 musicians.[63]

So what is an arts organization to do in such an economy-conscious world? Partner with organizations to cut costs, share audience, find corporate partners, and create consortiums. Scheff and Kotler may not endorse a war on waste per se but do certainly recommend a war on duplication and overspending.

> If arts organizations are careful to select appropriate collaborators, if collaborators have similar or complementary goals, and if the relationship is managed successfully, strategic collaborations can help participants achieve their organizational goals and better manage their financial, human, and physical resources. In this way, arts organizations will better realize their own mission and better serve their customers, their partners, and their communities as a whole. This is no small accomplishment for organizations struggling to survive as vital institutions in a rapidly changing environment.[64]

The argument almost works, but the repeated references to customers and business models may create a disconnect with the basic stewardship function that arts organizations play in their communities. Such is the challenge of pulling business models across the sectoral boundaries. Would that business gurus learned a few synonyms for customer; for example, patrons, clients, or citizens. And would that they figured out how to make the case around mission instead of simple cost savings.

Unfortunately, lacking alternatives to traditional business definitions of organizational effectiveness, nonprofit advocates are often forced to make the case for reform using the language of commercialism (customers, profits, business process reengineering) that is so often offensive to the sector they seek to help.

The case for restructuring can be made in more compelling terms, however. David La Piana tried to do so in a lengthy report on strategic restructuring for the James Irvine Foundation only a year or so after the *Harvard Business Review* published two more articles on the subject. Although funders are his intended audience, La Piana's *Beyond Collaboration: Strategic Restructuring of Nonprofit Organizations* is easily accessible to nonprofit boards and their chief professional officers.

With twenty years of nonprofit consulting experience, La Piana is no stranger to the sector. His report is both sensitive and tough regarding the need to act. But he also is convinced that the sector can learn from business and draws repeated analogies to the reputed success of corporate reengineering. "Likely nonprofit candidates for strategic restructuring are analogous to businesses with under-valued stock: the necessary elements for success are present, but the organization needs outside help to move it forward. When a business's restructuring is successful, its stock value rises dramatically. When a nonprofit's restructuring is successful, its ability to fulfill its social mission rises dramatically."[65]

His definition of strategic restructuring is distinguished from the more familiar, and perhaps more intimidating, business process reengineering, by its evolutionary nature. Nonprofits need not merge into newly created organizations to engage in strategic restructuring. They can enter into joint ventures, back-office consolidations, and intermediary financial relationships of one kind or another.

Toward that more flexible embrace, La Piana gives the funding community a simple list of questions that the sector must ask itself as it considers restructuring: (1) how can the options for nonprofit strategic restructuring be best defined and described, (2) is the climate right for strategic restructuring and will it improve the functioning of the individual nonprofits, (3) what pressures lead nonprofits to consider mergers, consolidations, and joint ventures, and what difficulties prevent them from bringing these efforts to fruition, (4) how can funders encourage nonprofits to undertake strategic restructuring without being perceived as applying pressure to do so, and (5) what educational activities can funders promote to encourage strategic restructuring activities?

No matter how thoughtfully presented, however, strategic restructuring is still driven by the same competitive pressure that led Hammer to author his famous "Don't Automate, Obliterate" call for reengineering.[66] Thus, La Piana opens his report with a blunt assessment of what nonprofits must do to succeed at strategic alliances: "The challenge confronting nonprofits is to look beyond collaboration—to build sustainable, long-term relationships that fundamentally change the way they function as organizations. . . . These undertakings are not easily achieved. They require nonprofit leaders to yield some of their autonomy, to make themselves vulnerable and to open their organizational cultures to outside influences. In return, these efforts have saved essential nonprofit services (if not the organizations that originally delivered them) from extinction, resulted in an improved market position, and opened the door to new opportunities."[67] It is a very tough message but has the attractive attribute of focusing on mission, not profit, as the driver for implementation.

The question, therefore, is how funders can encourage restructuring without frightening the organizations they seek to help. The Maryland Association of Nonprofit Organizations may have found one way to make restructuring more palatable through its new Management Innovation Fund (MI Fund). Created in 1998, the fund challenged corporate and foundation supporters to put up or shut up; that is, put up dollars for strategic restructuring or stop complaining about waste and inefficiency among Maryland nonprofits. The result is a fund designed to provide technical assistance to support strategic restructuring among small and medium-size nonprofits. Over its first two years, the MI Fund has supported a wide range of projects, including at least two mergers, several partnerships, and a growing number of organizational assessments. By offering technical assistance grants ranging from $10,000 to $100,000, the MI Fund has been particularly successful in getting boards of individual organizations to open the search for partnerships, largely because the fund is managed by and for nonprofits, thereby insulating nonprofits from funder pressure. The grants are only available through a competitive process that asks a given applicant for detailed information on basic motivation and hoped-for results.[68]

The great strength of war on waste is its focus on cost savings and efficiency. There is also no question, for example, that the MI Fund has produced more effective delivery of services, whether through the newly created Maryland Center for Community Development, Center for Poverty

Solutions, or the Big Brothers–Big Sisters of Baltimore-Maryland Mentoring Partnership.

The weakness of war on waste is its focus on cost savings and efficiency as the core measurement of success and the possible reduction in innovation as a result. Consider the notion that the problem in the arts community is not so much the lack of audience, but the supply of orchestras, a point made in the opening paragraph of Scheff and Kotler's *Harvard Business Review* article. Is it a problem that the number of orchestras "swelled from 58 to more than 1,000" between the 1960s and 1980s? Is it a problem that the number of professional resident theater companies "increased from 12 to more than 400"? And is it a problem that, by 1987, "ticket revenues for nonprofit performing arts organizations exceeded ticket revenues for sporting events"? In this regard, the missing question of La Piana's analysis of strategic restructuring is how funders can strike a balance between too many organizations and too few. To be fair, La Piana's work is not about reducing the total number of nonprofits, but about giving funders a new set of tools to enhance efficiency. Nevertheless, La Piana's use of business reengineering rhetoric at the start of the report could be read as a signal that fewer is better.

The nonprofit sector would also do well to assess the current state of corporate reengineering before it fully embraces restructuring. "Reengineering didn't start out as a code word for mindless bloodshed," one of its early boosters, Thomas H. Davenport, wrote only five years after Hammer's famous call to action. "It wasn't supposed to be the last gasp of Industrial Age management. . . . I explicitly said that using it for cost reduction alone was not a sensible goal. And consultants Michael Hammer and James Champy, the two names most closely associated with reengineering, have insisted all along that layoffs shouldn't be the point. But the fact is, once out of the bottle, the reengineering genie quickly turned ugly."[69] As Davenport argues, reengineering has been a mixed success at best. It may produce higher stock values when successful, as La Piana argues, but it may not be very successful overall.

Therein lies the potential for lost productivity. Like a Gary Larsen "Far Side" cartoon, when workers hear the words *restructuring*, *strategic alliance*, or even *collaboration*, they may think *unemployment*. That is why the MI Fund represents such a breakthrough in encouraging needed restructuring. When coupled with the Maryland Standards for Excellence, the MI Fund gives local nonprofits the power to improve themselves by looking to their internal processes and by embracing the outside world. As such, it may also be the most powerful example of how foundations can engage in what Christine Letts, William Ryan, and Allen Grossman call "venture philanthropy," a model of fundgiving that encourages foundations to invest more deeply in the core capacities of the organizations they support.[70]

Before leaving the discussion of collaboration, it is important to note the general imprecision surrounding use of the term. Collaboration may be one of those rare and celebrated goals of organizational life, but it can mean everything from minimal information sharing to full-blown merger. As my former colleague at the Pew Charitable Trusts Elizabeth Hubbard argues, "The idea of working together through partnerships is talked about so frequently that the word 'partner' has been adopted as a verb, as in 'we'll partner with other agencies.' "[71]

Whether a partnership involves full blown *collaboration*, which Hubbard defines as a form of collective problem solving that blurs the lines between agencies and La Piana would call strategic alliance, *cooperation*, which involves common, but separate, action to meet a mutual goal such as the MI Fund's Big Brothers–Big Sisters of Baltimore mentoring project, or *coordination*, which involves a more limited sharing of resources to assist other agencies, information is a key resource. Nonprofits may have to choose between keeping secrets or making partners.

The three types vary by the degree of power sharing—cooperation involves less, collaboration much more. Moreover, within each of the three types of partnership are different levels of resource involvement—sharing information is relatively cheap; sharing resources is more expensive. The combination of type and resource commitment produces nine relatively discrete forms of partnership (see figure 3-1). The bottom left cell (sharing information) would be the least costly form of partnership, while the top right cell (sharing program responsibilities) would be the most costly.

Just because the term is ill-defined does not mean that collaboration is a wasted effort. To the contrary, collaboration is attractive to reformers because it seems to improve performance under a variety of circumstances. That is one of the lessons in my book *Sustaining Innovation: Creating Government and Nonprofit Organizations That Innovate Naturally.* Virtually all of the twenty-six organizations I defined as innovating organizations engaged in one or more of the nine forms of partnership defined in figure 3-1—sometimes sharing information to eliminate duplication,

Figure 3-1. Forms of Partnerships

		Type of partnership	
	Cooperation	Coordination	Collaboration
High	*Contributing resources* Agencies contribute resources to another agency's project or effort; contribution is clearly defined and usually material.	*Reconciling activities* Agencies adjust or combine existing programs to deliver services more effectively; usually entails ongoing relationships among partners.	*Sharing program responsibilities* Agencies come together as a new entity to provide services or to manage a resource.
Level of resource involvement	*Promoting others* Agencies willingly share information about the work or services of others.	*Sharing resources or programs* Agencies that use the same good or service agree to share in its cost; often defined by contract.	*Creating new systems* Agencies work to create and implement a new model to deliver services or address a public problem.
Low	*Sharing information* Agencies share information on a formal or informal basis.	*Producing joint projects* Agencies depend upon each other for producing a specific product or event; generally involves short-term commitments.	*Planning collectively* Agencies develop a vision or conduct a study for the management of a resource or the alleviation of a social problem.

other times sharing resources to reduce costs, and still other times joining together for collective planning.[72]

Because the decision to engage in what La Piana calls strategic restructuring or what others call partnering depends on circumstance and opportunity, reformers must do more than just call for more activity. They must also specify the conditions under which one or another form of partnership advances an organization's mission. As organizations move up and across the inventory of partnering options, they must use great care in determining the best alternatives for their changing circumstances. Unfortunately, the science of strategic alliances has some distance to go before it can become a hard and fast recommendation for action. And that involves at least some further research on which forms of working together are most appropriate under what circumstances for which kind of nonprofit organizations.

Watchful Eye

Watchful eye is one of the most powerful traditions in management reform of any kind. It is based on the elementary belief that the sunshine of public scrutiny, be it applied to corporate earning reports, the federal administrative process, or nonprofit financial statements, is the most powerful disinfectant available. The notion is that organizations will not behave unethically if they know that citizens and the media might be watching. By throwing open the curtains that have so long protected corruption, advocates of watchful eye expect shame, embarrassment, and citizen pressure to do the work that scientific management and its legion of rules fail to do. (Box 3-3 summarizes the key characteristics of watchful eye.)

The defining expression of watchful eye in government is the Administrative Procedure Act, which was enacted in 1946. The act was designed around four basic themes that arise in virtually every effort to open organizations to public inspection. One can cut and paste the legislative rationale for the act and easily capture the flavor of the tide as it applies to the nonprofit sector today:

(1) To require agencies [nonprofits] to keep the public currently informed of their organization, procedures, and rules.

(2) To provide for public participation in the rulemaking [fundgiving] process.

Box 3-3. *Characteristics of Watchful Eye*

Common expression: Transparency

Central assumption: Making financial and performance information visible will allow competition to weed out inefficiency

Focus: External visibility

Primary implementors: Individual donors

Accountability model: Compliance on releasing information, performance on content

Cost of implementation: Low on release, high on generating performance information

Time to higher performance: Short if information is raw, long if information must improve

Measurability of change: High

Level of independence: Low to high

Stress on organization: Low

Patron saint: Ralph Nader

Patron organization: GuideStar

Strengths: Openness, donor empowerment

Weaknesses: Inaccuracy, manipulation

---

(3) To prescribe uniform standards for the conduct of formal rulemaking and adjudicatory proceedings [solicitation of funds].

(4) To restate the law of judicial review [the authority of donors].[73]

Congress chose not to attach a code of conduct to the original Administrative Procedures Act. The point was to open the process to inspection, not to discipline rulemakers. The decision to reject an ethics code reflected a deep concern among reformers that such codes tend to "become merely hortatory." As President Franklin D. Roosevelt's Committee on Administrative Procedure chastised such efforts, codes either "appear to prescribe a uniform procedure and to erect standards; but, in fact, and in application, they dissolve and permit whatever in the opinion of the administrator is practicable and necessary" or command "the obvious, in situations where obedience of the command will, without the code, vitiate administrative action." Codes tend to say either " 'do as you please' or 'do nothing which is lawless,'" neither of which is likely to improve accountability.

Once enacted, the Administrative Procedure Act spawned a long list of sunshine statutes, including the Federal Advisory Committee Act, which requires that all meetings be open to the public, the Government in the Sunshine Act, which opens the administrative process to deeper review, and the Freedom of Information Act, which allows individual citizens and reporters to request the release of classified and unclassified materials. Without dwelling on the role of such statutes in creating what New York Democratic senator Daniel Patrick Moynihan has labeled a "culture of government secrecy," the laws undoubtedly have raised public expectations of transparency across the sectors.

If the purpose of these statutes was to stimulate the release of information, they have succeeded beyond their authors' wildest dreams. The amount of data produced by government is staggering. In this regard, Regina E. Herzlinger's notion that government needs to release more information to earn greater public confidence is wrong. A good argument could be made that government needs to write fewer reports and release less information. What Herzlinger is concerned about is not so much the quantity of information, but the quality: "Currently there is little disclosure of performance information for nonprofit and governmental organizations, especially measures of effectiveness such as client satisfaction. Financial information is often lacking as well." The news is even worse from the nonprofit sector: "Although the Internal Revenue Service requires financial statements and some compensation and outcome disclosure from exempt organizations in an annual return called Form 990, the disclosure has been of such poor quality that the attorney general of Connecticut found that two-thirds of the forms filed contained at least one arithmetic error. The U.S. General Accounting Office found that half of those they reviewed were missing at least one of the required supporting schedules."[74] Herzlinger is also right to complain about the lack of systematic analysis and dissemination of most of the information collected.

But whether disclosure, analysis, dissemination, and sanctions for the failure to disclose properly would improve performance is an entirely different matter. Some emerging data, for example, suggest that the more some consumers know about government agencies, the less confidence they have. According to a 1998 survey of customer satisfaction of five federal agencies, the impact of personal contact on trust depended on which agency was contacted. As the Pew Research Center for the People and the Press found, the more personal contact citizens have with the Social Security Administration, the less satisfied they are, largely because they start out thinking so highly of the agency that contact can only disappoint. At the same time, the more contact citizens have with the Internal Revenue Service, the more satisfied they are, no doubt because they start out thinking so poorly of the agency that contact can only surprise.[75]

Moreover, good evidence is available that what matters most to raising trust in government is performance, not the availability of information. Americans are notoriously disconnected from the day-to-day business of government, and by implication the nonprofit sector, but they do have general impressions on how well the Postal Service or the Centers for Disease Control and Prevention are doing in delivering the goods, or how well the Environmental Protection Agency and Social Security Administration are doing in serving the public.[76]

This is not to suggest that watchful eye cannot be a lever for improvement when linked to changes in what organizations must report. Hence, the disclosure of performance information depends in large measure on getting organizations to think carefully about mission and results. Unfortunately, the early experience with the Government Performance and Results Act has been less than encouraging. Federal agencies have had great difficulty implementing the cumbersome statute, which is filled with compliance-based instructions on what constitutes a goal, outcome, measurable result, and so forth but offers little reward for agencies to link those measures to the things that matter most to the delivery of goods and services—dollars and staff.

The most aggressive promoter of watchful eye is GuideStar, the Richmond organization that is providing the backbone of helping.org in collaboration with America Online. GuideStar intends to make every Form 990 available online and opened a Washington, D.C., office in May 1999, headed by a former National Science Foundation inspector general, to pursue its vision of a national system of electronic Form 990 filing.

GuideStar is not alone in the effort. With funding in part from the Mellon Foundation, the National Center for Charitable Statistics (NCCS) at the Urban Institute is also investing in improved information delivery, including a draft Universal Data Element Dictionary (U-DED), to generate more than two hundred data elements on every nonprofit organization in the United States. Headed by the founding director of the Aspen Institute's Nonprofit Sector Research Fund, NCCS sees its mission as nothing less than a "revolution in access to data," which, in turn, "creates an opportunity for a strategic sector-wide intervention to ensure that all the affected groups work together to create uniform data standards and reports that paint a reliable portrait of the sector."[77]

The implementors of watchful eye are not big organizations, funders, or even Internet information providers, but ordinary citizens who must know enough to make careful choices. Citizens cannot know enough, however, unless they know their rights to information, which is why GuideStar summarizes the "Donor's Bill of Rights" on its website. According to the bill of rights, which was developed by the American Association of Fund-Raising Counsel, the Association for Healthcare Philanthropy, the Council for Advancement and Support of Education, and the National Society of Fund-Raising Executives and endorsed by Independent Sector, the National Catholic Development Conference, the National Committee on Planned Giving, and the United Way of America, information is the key to respect and confidence. Toward that end, a donor has the right to:

1. Be informed of the organization's mission, of the way the organization intends to use donated resources, and of its capacity to use donations effectively for their intended purposes.

2. Be informed of the identity of those serving on the organization's governing board, and to expect the board to exercise prudent judgment in its stewardship responsibilities.

3. Have access to the organization's most recent financial statements.

4. Be assured that their gifts will be used for the purposes for which they were given.

5. Receive appropriate acknowledgment and recognition.

6. Be assured that information about their donations is handled with respect and with confidentiality to the fullest extent provided by the law.

7. Expect that all relationships with individual representing organizations of interest to the donor will be professional in nature.

8. Be informed whether those seeking donations are volunteers, employees of the organization or hired solicitors.

9. Have the opportunity for their names to be deleted from mailing lists that an organization intends to share.

10. Feel free to ask questions when making a donation and to receive prompt, truthful, and forthright answers.[78]

No one could question the merits of such a watchful system or the responsibility of individual donors to ask hard questions about their giving dollars. But the transparency is not without costs.

Some evidence has emerged, for example, that the disclosure rules created under the "Tax Payer Bill of Rights" can be exploited to so inundate a given nonprofit with information requests that it is unable to operate. Although organizations do not have to provide copies of their Form 990s if the documents are widely available or if the organization is a target of a harassment campaign, nonprofits must apply to the Internal Revenue Service to seek the needed determination. The rules are complicated enough, however, to create a new branch of nonprofit law dealing expressly with the Form 990, which is one way in which all four tides of reform eventually create that sediment of rules that can impede organizational performance in their own right.

Nonprofits are already working to use the new disclosure rules to present a positive face to the public. Information is never neutral, after all, a point reinforced by the Independent Sector's "Giving Voice to Your Heart" outreach campaign. Although not linked directly to the Form 990 issue, the campaign speaks to the sector's desire to shape information. Launched in 1998 following extensive research on public attitudes, the campaign features three basic themes: (1) "America's nonprofit organizations make a difference in the lives of people, our communities, our country, and the world," (2) "The nonprofit sector puts our shared values into action—values such as compassion, altruism, democracy, pluralism, and freedom of expression, religion, and association," and (3) "Citizen involvement is what makes the nonprofit sector work."[79] The campaign is no different from hundreds that Washington trade associations mount each year, which is exactly the point. It even comes with materials that allow an association or individual nonprofit to customize the campaign for local consumption, including a suggested action list, letter to the editor, talking points, press release, op-ed, and speech.

It is also a point made on the Minnesota Council of Nonprofits webpage, which encourages nonprofits to offer more than just financials when someone requests the Form 990. "What next?" the Council asks. Start with a cover that makes a good first impression, including an "attitude of welcoming accountability and interest in your agency"; get to know readers by providing more information than they want; throw in "context, good dialogue, characters, foreshadowing, a compelling mission" alongside the required information and indicate "your stance on accountability; welcome future requests and feedback." The result: a possible "best seller" that makes the case for the organization even as it satisfies the rules.[80]

Finally, one reason for the concern about common data is the potential for manipulation of information by unscrupulous nonprofits. Despite the best efforts of accounting standards boards and watchdog groups to ferret out misinformation, financial statements can sometimes seem more art than scientific management. One of the early concerns with the GuideStar reporting system was its proposed inventory of standard financial indicators built off the Form 990 reports. Although one can easily calculate a fund-raising or administrative cost to operating or program expenditure ratio, the Form 990 data are so unreliable that such an indicator would be more a guide to an organization's cleverness perhaps than any real commitment to precision or consistency. As one funder argues, the Form 990s as currently filed combine "applies, organizes, and kiwis." Would that the advocates of greater Form 990 compliance also determine whether the document asks the right questions.

Ultimately, it is not clear how aggressive monitoring agencies such as GuideStar and the Better Business Bureau can be without the active participation of the nonprofit sector. Of the twenty-three organizations rated by the Council of Better Business Bureaus' Philanthropic Advisory Service in October 1999, for example, seven fully met the standards, six failed to meet one or more of the standards, and eight did not provide enough information to be rated at all.[81] It may yet turn out that the transparency movement fades because of a lack of interest and participation. Donors may not ask, and nonprofits may not tell.

Liberation Management

At first blush, liberation management appears to be the anti-tide, meaning that it represents a general effort to undo and dismantle the rules and structures associated with scientific management, war on waste, and watchful eye. This reputation comes largely from association with Gore's

---

Box 3-4. *Characteristics of Liberation Management*

Common expression: Deregulation, outcomes management, employee empowerment

Central assumption: Organizations should focus on results, not rules, and be entrepreneurial

Focus: Internal freedom and competitiveness

Primary implementors: Individual employees and organizations

Accountability model: Performance as general goal, compliance on specific implementation

Cost of implementation: Low to high depending upon density of rules and structure

Time to higher performance: Low to high depending upon density of rules and structure

Measurability of change: Low to moderate

Level of independence: Very high

Stress on organization: Low

Patron saint: Al Gore

Patron organization: United Way of America

Strengths: Focus on measurable progress toward mission

Weaknesses: Potential loss of discipline, focus on wrong "customers"

---

reinventing government campaign, which made a simple case on behalf of liberation: "The federal government is filled with good people trapped in bad systems; budget systems, personnel systems, procurement systems, financial management systems. When we blame the people and impose more controls, we make the systems worse."[82] (See box 3-4 for the characteristics of liberation management.)

Whether applied to government or the nonprofit sector, liberation management derives much of its inspiration from David Osborne and Ted Gaebler's best-selling book *Reinventing Government: How the Entrepreneurial Spirit Is Transforming the Public Sector*, which, in turn, draws upon a broad range of general interest best sellers, most visibly including Tom Peters and Richard Waterman's *In Search of Excellence*.[83] With Osborne as its author in chief, Gore's first reinventing report featured four broad themes that echoed *Reinventing Government*: (1) "Cutting Red Tape," which included budget streamlining, decentralization of the personnel process, efforts to reorienting the inspectors general toward a more cooperative posture, and empowering state and local governments; (2) "Putting Customers First," which focused on the use of the market to discipline government, whether through increased outsourcing or interagency competition, alongside a commitment to measuring results; (3) "Empowering Employees to Get Results," which centered on giving employees more authority to do their work without interference, and (4) "Cutting Back to Basics," which emphasized a standard package of budget cuts, productivity investments, and modest reengineering.

Despite the use of contemporary terms such as empowerment, Osborne and Gore's liberation management is hardly a new idea. Thomas Jefferson articulated many of the Osborne principles at one time or another during his long public career. According to administrative historian Lynton Caldwell, Jefferson believed in harmony among employees (hence would likely support the call for labor-management partnership), simplicity (hence would likely endorse cutting back to basics), and adaptability (hence would likely endorse greater flexibility for agencies). Most important, Jefferson believed in decentralization of power, reflecting both a personal preference for local control and what Caldwell labels "a highly subjective distrust of professionalized administration and complex administrative machinery."[84]

Central to liberation management is the dual notion that (1) employees know best about what works and (2) that accountability resides in careful measurement of results not endless checklists and oversight. Liberation management involves a clear trade-off between the old compliance accountability of scientific management and the new performance accountability of outcomes measurement. Employees, and the organizations in which they reside, can be free to do their jobs only if their work enhances results. Hence the title of Gore's first report: *From Red-Tape to Results*.

This is not to argue that liberation management has no interest in compliance. To the contrary, the implementation of the Government Performance and Results Act of 1993 has produced a thicket of definitions and procedures. The act, which can be traced back to the Defense Department's Program, Planning, and Budgeting System (PPBS) from the 1960s, has spawned an entire industry of consultants whose sole job, it

seems, is to teach the federal government the language and rules of outcomes measurement. Even the effort to free agencies from the rules produces more rules.[85]

Consider the July 1998 revision of Budget Circular A-11 as an example. Alongside thirty-four pages of definitions for key terms in the
Government Performance and Results Act statute (general goal, general
objective, outcome goal, output goal, performance goal, performance
indicator, program activity, program evaluation), the circular provided a
detailed timetable governing all submissions of initial, updated, revised,
and interim strategic plans that form the backbone of measurement
process, as well as formal instructions regarding the formatting of documents, transmittal of materials, deadlines, coding rules, principles for
choosing program indicators, and verification and validation methodologies. Unfortunately, as the following definitions may suggest, the Circular
did little to clarify the key terms that drive the outcomes movement. Even
with the details, agencies could hardly be faulted for being confused
about what the Office of Management and Budget (OMB) and Congress
might have intended. The following definitions of general goals and general objectives serve as an example:

> General goal: Included in a strategic plan, this goal defines how
> an agency will carry out its mission over a specific period of time.
> The goal is expressed in a manner which allows a future assessment
> to be made of whether the goal was or is being achieved. The goal
> may be of a programmatic, policy, or managemental [sic] nature.
> General goals are predominantly outcome-type goals.
>
> General objective: Included in a strategic plan, the objective(s)
> are paired with a general goal, and can be used to help assess
> whether a general goal was or is being achieved. An objective usu-
> ally describes a more specific level of achievement than a general
> goal.
>
> Outcome goal: A description of the intended result, effect, or con-
> sequence that will occur from carrying out a program or activity.
>
> Output goal: A description of the level of activity or effort that
> will be produced over a period of time or by a specified date, includ-
> ing a description of the characteristics and attributes (e.g., timeli-
> ness) established as standards in the course of conducting the activ-
> ity or effort.[86]

Much as one is tempted to replace the list with the United Way of America's much simpler glossary, the bureaucratese betrays the Office of Management and Budget's own ambivalence about outcomes management. After all, an outcomes system would render the budget office little more than a rubber stamp for agency-determined priorities. By making implementation as difficult as possible, the agency assures its continued dominance in budget politics. And that kind of politics is sometimes why reform does not stick.

The nonprofit sector has not adopted every element of Gore's liberation management. So much authority is found at the bottom of many nonprofit organizations that no need exists to talk of empowerment. Much of the stress in the sector is caused by what some might characterize as overempowerment: too much work, not enough money, and not enough operating support. Nevertheless, the nonprofit sector or its funders or both have embraced at least two of the key elements of liberation management: outcomes measurement and competition.

No national organization has been more engaged in the outcome measurement effort than the United Way of America. Its Task Force on Impact began working in August 1995 on strengthening outcomes measurement in the field. At the time, only twenty-five to thirty local United Ways were engaged in any form of outcomes measurement, which the United Way of America defines as an evolutionary process that starts with a general commitment to change and moves step by step through agency training, identifying program outcomes and indicators, collecting data, communicating with donors, using the data, linking program outcomes to indicators of community change, and measuring community change. Of those twenty-five to thirty, only two or three had enough outcome data to use for making funding decisions.[87]

Three hundred local United Ways were somewhere up the change ladder three years later, in no small part because of the tireless promotion by the national organization and the onslaught of information and technical assistance on how to do outcomes measurement. By 1999, the United Way of America could boast of thirty lessons learned over the years, many of which stress the need to let individual agencies define their outcomes, while making clear that the reform is both doable and inevitable:

Nonprofit agencies often ask if outcome measurement is just a fad that, if ignored long enough, will go away. The consensus of the

field is a resounding "No." Like earlier aspects of performance measurement that built upon each other to strengthen the management
and delivery of nonprofit services, the careful measurement of outcomes is another essential building block that informs us in new
and necessary ways about how to improve programs. It is not the
last brick to be added. Nor has it developed as far as it can and will.
However, outcome measurement is here to stay, and the nonprofit
sector and the individuals it serves will be the better for it.[88]

Despite all the evidence the United Way of America provides, not the
least of which is the use of outcomes measurement in accreditation
processes, there is a certain "whistling past the graveyard" tone to the
promotion. Anyone familiar with outcomes measurement knows that the
idea has been floating through government and the nonprofit sector for
decades, occasionally rising in specific initiatives such as PPBS, President
Gerald R. Ford's management by objectives (MBO), and President Jimmy
Carter's zero-based budgeting (ZBB), only to fade again as hope confronts
the difficulty of management. At least for now, the latest federal effort is
starting to stagnate as agencies struggle with basic definitions and the
enormous amount of paperwork involved, and they await the 2000 elec-
tion to see if the next president shares Gore's commitment to reform.

The future of an outcomes-based liberation may still be in doubt, but
the marketization of nonprofit services is most certainly not. Private competition appears here to stay, as does the growing effort by individual
nonprofits to produce their own revenue. Much of this pressure comes
directly from the federal government, which has endorsed competition as
a device for improving front-line performance—be it in schools, government agencies, or nonprofits. It was a point President Bill Clinton made
in signing the Government Management Reform Act of 1994, an otherwise obscure statute to encourage more competition in contracting:
"Injecting competition and market forces into the delivery of these services will reduce duplication, lower overhead costs, and better serve the
American people." And it was a point he made later the same year in
demanding that all departments and agencies develop customer service
standards, creating the illusion of a market for agencies that could not or
would not compete.[89]

No one knows how far the marketization will go, if only because it is
proceeding one state and locality at a time and is poorly tracked. The best
one can do is monitor the latest examples, which appear here and there

on the web, and ask hard questions about who is doing what for whom at what cost and consequence.

Take the 1998 marketization of San Diego County's welfare-to-work services as an example. Scholars know that the county divided its Department of Social Services into Family Resource Centers, which are now located in six geographical regions. They also know that the county entered into outcomes-based contracts with four providers: remnants of the county's old welfare-to-work staff, Lockheed Martin IMS, Maximus, and Catholic Charities. Finally, scholars know that the Metropolitan Area Advisory Committee, a nonprofit consortium in South Bay, San Diego, challenged the Maximus bid and lost, and that a group of welfare recipients and former county employees filed suit in August 1999 seeking to cancel the contracts. Although the suit was dismissed, it does send a warning that government employee unions are willing to fight privatization to private or nonprofit organizations.

That is the extent of the information. As with much of the marketization around the country, be it in Milwaukee County where Maximus won a three-year $24 million welfare-to-work contract from the state or the District of Columbia where Lockheed Martin IMS won a similar $33 million contract, San Diego is merely a story with few links to any prevailing wisdom on the long-term impacts of the market-based version of liberation management. [90]

Of particular interest in the San Diego case is the county's decision not to evaluate this natural experiment. The county's sole focus is on the end results of the contracts. The contractor or contractors who produce the most placements will presumably win a consolidated contract when the current experiment expires in 2001. In theory, it should not matter whether a recipient receives her or his welfare training from Lockheed Martin IMS or Catholic Charities, the county's staff or Maximus. In reality, no evaluation system is in place to ask why or how outcomes vary, or to examine the long-term impacts of privatization on San Diego County's civic health.

Little other available evidence points to a rapid expansion of competition as Temporary Assistance to Needy Families (TANF) takes hold. Passed in 1996 as a promised end to the existing state of welfare, the act gave state and local government broad authority to contract out to private and nonprofit organizations. According to the Welfare Information Network, which has been monitoring privatization on an ad hoc basis, marketization is either under way or under active consideration in

California, Colorado (where the final TANF implementation rule gives counties explicit authority to contract out), Florida (where state law requires full privatization of all welfare programs except for food stamps and medicaid eligibility determination), Indiana, Massachusetts, Michigan (where local agencies are required to contract out all school-to-work and welfare-to-work services), New York, Oklahoma, Pennsylvania (where the state has assembled a wide range of private, nonprofit, government agencies, and faith-based organizations to provide its welfare-to-work services), Texas (where the state has proposed full privatization of all welfare services, including eligibility determination), Washington, and Wisconsin (where the state requires competitive bidding when a local government agency fails to meet specific performance targets).[91] Although most of this privatization is sector-neutral regarding who gets the contract, the demand for information management tends to favor private contractors such as Lockheed Martin IMS or Electronic Data Systems (EDS), which can bring extraordinary technological capacity to the bidding process.

Although there is a certain inevitability to much of the marketization discussion, not everyone is comfortable with the trend. Edward Skloot, executive director of the Surdna Foundation, has made privatization a feature of recurring concern in both his speeches and grantmaking. Although no one can predict exactly how far the current marketization will go, he sees the impact of the recent welfare outsourcing:

> First, if local governments squeeze the profit margins in their contracts in each bidding cycle, they can kill off the competitors the new law has attracted. Squeezing profit margins will retard creativity and productivity. It will deeply hurt the people welfare reform is designed to help. A second nightmare scenario may already be here. Because the marketplace lets in new entrants easily, companies increasingly low-ball their bids in order to gain a toe-hold. For example, cut-throat competition has overtaken Electronic Benefits Transfers. This is the way welfare clients gain their benefits, from food stamps to child support.[92]

So do Laurie Paarlberg and Kristen Gronbjerg, who evaluated the rise of nonprofit fee-for-service income on behalf of the Aspen Institute's Nonprofit Strategy Group and concluded that the continued blurring of the line between nonprofit and private sector "is likely to become a focus of public policy debate, raising questions about the need to continue to subsidize nonprofit organizations through preferential tax treatment."[93] Mark Rosenman and Kristin Scotchmer are even tougher in another report prepared for the Strategy Group: "It is widely acknowledged that the market's growth and diffusion fuels its further expansion. Developments during the past couple of decades demonstrate that absent conscious and concerted effort in another direction, the market will infuse ever increasing areas of nonprofit operation. If commercialization continues unabated, how can we look at the nonprofit sector as an instrument of civil society and public purpose? There is a choice to be made."[94]

The antimarketization pressure is not just coming from the nonprofit sector. The American Federation of State, County, and Municipal Employees (AFSCME), which represents 1.3 million state and local government employees, has made privatization a top issue, reserving the cover of its January 1998 *Public Employee* magazine for a story titled "Raiders of the Lost Jobs." "Whether you live in a large city or a small town," the story began, "there's a corporate executive with an eye on your job. Billion-dollar corporate raiders with names like Lockheed Martin IMS, Marriott International and Corrections Corporation of America see potential profits in every jail, school cafeteria, welfare office, health clinic and landfill. . . . From city to city, state to state, AFSCME members are confronting these corporate giants: keeping services in public hands wherever possible, fighting for collective bargaining agreements when it's not. And AFSCME members in communities across the country have even beaten these Goliaths at their own game, they have shown that unionized public workers can get the job done faster, cheaper and better."[95] AFSCME hardly cares about the nonprofit sector. It opposes any contracting out, whether to privates or nonprofits.

Despite this opposition, anyone who doubts the growing market for marketization need only attend one of the dozens of business training programs offered regularly and to full attendance by private firms such as the Institute for International Research (IIR). Nonprofit executives attending IIR's December 1999 "Innovative Business Strategies for Non Profit Organizations" event were treated to two days dealing with "New Competitive Realities," "Thrilling the Customer," "Unleashing New Resources and Building a Network of Social Entrepreneurs," "Building a Great Non Profit Brand," "Creating a Brand Identity," "Seeking Out Non-Traditional Sources of Income," "Beyond On-Line Giving: On-Line Campaigning," and "Partnering with For Profit Organizations." The speakers were hardly business hacks drawn to a new audience. They were senior leaders in the field such as Jim Pitofsky, vice president of the echoing green foundation, Thomas K. Reis, venture philanthropist director at the Kellogg Foundation, and Trabian Shorters, the circuit rider from the Meyer Foundation.[96]

Nor can anyone doubt that nonprofits will remain under pressure to become more businesslike and entrepreneurial. As an environmental scan funded and directed by the Kellogg Foundation suggests, the nonprofit innovation is driven by two forces. "First, the nature of the desired social change often benefits from an innovative, entrepreneurial, or enterprise-based solution," write Reis and Stephanie J. Clohesy. "Second, the sustainability of the organization and its services requires diversification of its funding streams, often including the creation of earned income streams or a partnership with a for-profit."[97] Driven in part by what Gregory Dees calls the "pro-business zeitgeist" across the world, and frustration and fatigue with project fund-raising, nonprofits cannot be faulted for wanting to control their own destiny.

Whether and how that desire fits with the other tides, including the concern for greater transparency, is not clear. Watchful eye is predicated on the notion that there are no secrets, while entrepreneurship is built around the concept of intellectual property. Scientific management is centered on the concept of one best way, while entrepreneurship is rooted in "just do it!"

Whether nonprofits can "just do it" with current funding arrangements and accounting requirements is another question. Missing from the contemporary conversation about outcomes measurement is any mention of waivers from the traditional rules that funders impose on their grantees. Even as funders ask for more attention to outcomes, they do so without loosening the reporting requirements and financial disclosures. Grantees are asked to focus on outcomes by producing even more paperwork. It is one thing to talk about the need for liberation, and another to liberate nonprofit organizations from the rules that scientific management has produced over the years.

CHAPTER FOUR

The State
of theTides

The tides of nonprofit reform may share a general commitment to helping organizations improve, but they
are anything but uniform in method and intent. They proceed from different assumptions about what makes organizations work and exact different costs and place different stresses on their target organizations.

Lost in these differences are two characteristics that help sort the tides
into more meaningful categories. First, the four tides show different levels of trust in the organizations they seek to improve. Scientific and liberation management both put greater faith in the nonprofit sector to
improve itself given the proper guidance (standards) or incentives for success (performance and competition). Left to their own devices in this
increasingly turbulent world, nonprofits will seek to get better on their
own. All that advocates need to give them is a map.

In contrast, war on waste and watchful eye have less confidence in the
sector's ability to heal itself. Even the most hopeful advocate of mergers
and downsizing knows that external forces will largely supply the needed
discipline for action, while watchful eye has always had a distrusting tone
toward the organizations it seeks to improve. Left to their own devices,
advocates of the war on waste and watchful eye seem to say, nonprofits
will dodge the pressure to improve. Advocates have no choice but to com-
pel nonprofits to do the right thing.

Second, the four tides act at different levels of the sector. Scientific
management and war on waste tend to rely on concentrated authority to
enforce their recommendations, whether in the form of standard-setting

Figure 4-1. *Sorting the Tides*

		Trust in the nonprofit sector to implement reform	
		High	*Low*
Enforcement agents	*Concentrated*	Scientific management	War on waste
	Diffuse	Liberation management	Watchful eye

bodies such as the National Center for Charitable Statistics or state associations of nonprofits or funders. It is simply not in any organization's self-interest to pay attention to standards or merger opportunities absent concentrated authority. In contrast, liberation management and watchful eye look to much more diffuse sources of enforcement. Individual nonprofits must sense the market pressure and respond, or individual donors or reporters must find the websites and check the inventories of information. Absent interest within a relatively vast collection of possible enforcers, these two tides cannot succeed.

When these two dimensions are combined, one can easily sort the tides by their level of trust and enforcement strategy. There is a tide of reform for at least four separate persuasions (see figure 4-1). Those who have basic faith in the sector to improve itself, but also believe in the need for centralized enforcement, can turn to scientific management and its notion of a one best way, while those who have similar faith, but believe in letting a thousand flowers bloom, albeit under the same general pressure to produce and measure, can embrace liberation management and its notion of a sector rightly oriented to measurable mission. In contrast, those who have less confidence in the sector's willingness or self-interest in correcting itself and believe in strong control can turn to war on waste and its potential for sorting out the duplication, while those who share these doubts but who prefer a thousand flowers can find comfort in watchful eye and its ultimate army of donors and reporters.

Given these philosophical differences, nonprofits and funders caught in the competing tides might be uncertain as to the right choice. With so much reform coming from such different perspectives, nonprofits might be right to simply wait until something more comfortable and trusting comes along. After all, anyone dissatisfied with today's hot reform need only wait a year or two for something else to arrive.

Nonprofit management reforms do not die; they seem only to fade away for a time to return a few years later in a new package with a new push. Lacking hard research on what works and what does not, a particular reform movement can last forever.

This durability is apparent across the country. Not only is there a reform for every philosophy, but there is also a state somewhere in the nation where that tide is rising.

The Tides in the States

Even cursory contact with the states suggests that all four tides of nonprofit reform are active. Some ideas such as outcomes measurement may be rising, while others such as total quality management may be ebbing. But some organization somewhere in the vast nonprofit ocean is either just past the crest of a given tide or about to be hit by another. That is why the tides metaphor is so powerful. It speaks of the inevitability of change as ideas and reforms move in and out of prominence.

The metaphor also speaks to the realities reported by the nineteen state nonprofit associations contacted for this reconnaissance. Even though the associations are uneven in size and reputation, they offer a reasonable opportunity to take a snapshot of the tides as they move from coast to coast. Without claiming that their executive directors know everything that is happening to the roughly 300,000–400,000 nonprofits they represent, or the much smaller number of nonprofits that have joined their membership, the survey confirms many of the patterns discussed earlier in this report.[98]

For example, national and local scandals had taken their toll on the nonprofit sector, confirming the crisis of legitimacy. "If a private corporation like Boeing or IBM has a scandal, it doesn't color the whole private sector," one director of an eastern association argued. "But when something bad happens in the nonprofit sector, such as the United Way scandal, it sparks coverage everywhere. After the United Way scandal, our local paper turned on the nonprofit community and did a salary survey of nonprofits. The big story was a nonprofit executive who made more than $100,000 a year and drove a Lexus." The vast majority of the association directors echoed the complaint. Much as the rise of public or civic journalism offers a possible antidote, local news coverage has turned tougher toward charities as reporters look for new angles on the scandal story.

There was also frustration about the capacity to implement the wide range of reforms currently washing over William Ryan's new, market-driven landscape for nonprofits. "So many of our nonprofits 'just happened,'" another eastern director noted. "Our nonprofits are still evolving into real organizations, and are trying to get the basics right. To reengineer an organization, you'd need a plan, procedures, even an organization chart. Half of our nonprofits, it seems, don't even know what an organization chart looks like. And most aren't sure that getting one will make a bit of difference to what they do." Simply stated, reforming an organization is difficult when it has not yet been fully formed.

Finally, there was no doubt about pressure to become more businesslike, prompting at least one Midwestern director to complain about the "hundreds of nonprofit management centers posing as experts but really just recycling old business school cases and models. There are some common characteristics across the sectors, but we get hit by everything. If it works in business, or even if it doesn't, we're supposed to do it. The idea that nonprofits are well run only when they run like businesses is wrong." Most of the directors resisted the corporate language that sometimes gets mixed into the tides and often scoffed at the use of corporate terms such as *reengineering* or *total quality management*. At the same time, most of the directors recognized the inevitability of reform, and several expressed enthusiasm about the potential for making progress in professionalizing the sector through one reform tide or another.

Nevertheless, many of the states covered by the survey are embracing the businesslike pressure (see table 4-1). They may not like the corporate language and may resist the importation of corporate ideas for making their nonprofits work better, but they are adopting many of the core reforms outlined in this report. Although liberation management and war on waste were at their peak in the states, scientific management and watchful eye were both rising.

With scientific management, the standards movement has taken hold in both the east and Midwest and appears to be rising elsewhere as nonprofit associations adopt and refine the Maryland Association of Nonprofit Organizations model or come under pressure from the National Charities Information Bureau or the Better Business Bureau. All in all, however, support for standards is lukewarm at best, driven by a resignation more than a strong embrace.

Thus, some of the association directors saw standards as a natural defense against scandal. "We had three task forces working on standards

Table 4-1. *The Tides in the States*

Number of states

Tide	High tide	Rising tide	Low tide
Scientific management			
Standards	3	8	8
War on waste			
Reengineering, mergers	8	9	1
Watchful eye			
Transparency of Form 990	3	15	1
Liberation management			
Total quality management	0	1	17
Outcomes measurement	12	6	1
Marketization	2	10	6

in the mid 1990s, and eventually endorsed the BBB [Better Business Bureau] model," one western director noted. "The BBB had systems in place to handle queries and has links with law enforcement. It didn't make sense to create a separate system, but we needed some way to handle the spate of calls that always occur when we get a local or national scandal. It is one way to show progress."

Others viewed standards as a way to help their start-ups build the core capacity needed for further reform. "We have a lot of small nonprofits that need the basics," one southern director said. "They need some guidance on what they ought to do when they begin. Most of our new organizations have a ton of passion and deeply committed leaders, but they don't have a clue how to form a board or what to do about fundraising." Another southern director said his nonprofits "are growing up. First they were young teenagers and needed all this help on financial management, total quality management, and such. Now they're young adults and need to do more to act like it."

But most of the directors saw standards as a mixed blessing, fueling more of a neutrality than strong support or resistance. "We've looked at it," said one northeastern director, "but are not promoting it ourselves. Some of our subsectors are doing certification for day cares, and so forth, but really the content is not earthshaking or revolutionary. It is mostly codification of common sense. Whether it is worth all the hoopla is not clear." A southern director agreed. "Best practices and benchmarking are new to us, and our members love business language. But can you really get better by copying this stuff? It may be a meaningless exercise that gets you all the right words and manuals, but no real commitment. Our goal is to disseminate good things that are happening and let people know who they might contact to get into it. We don't think standards are the way to get there."

In contrast, the downsizings, mergers, and alliances of war on waste provoked intense allegiance or opposition. Although the word *reengineering* almost never comes up, some associations report intense interest in shared administrative services as a way to accommodate rapid growth in the nonprofit sector. "Reengineering comes up all the time in conferences and workshops, and our members love it," said one western director. "They'll come for it time and again. They are particularly interested in shared administrative services, but only if it starts inside the nonprofits themselves. No one likes it when some corporate type comes in to say this is how business does it best."

Other states report concern about future competition. "I don't hear the word *reengineering* here," said an eastern colleague. "There are lots of mergers, particularly in the health care area. Hospitals are taking over social services, mental health, substance abuse. The driver is that hospitals want to diversity and nonprofits want to survive. Nonprofits get economies of scale, security, and protection against future takeovers by for-profit business, and the hospitals get new revenue streams that they can use for cross-subsidies." An eastern director agreed: "We are ground zero of mergers. With the private sector coming into our state, it will be increasingly prevalent because of economies of scale."

Not all of the mergers are self-initiated, however. "*Reengineering* is not a term we use," said a southern director. "But we do a lot of mergers, partnerships, shared space, and so forth, mostly because funding sources (government and private), tell us to do so in order to get program money. That doesn't mean they'll pay for the costs, though. The only time a funder actually pays for the organizational change requested is when they come from out of state." Although most association directors reported a similar lack of funding, at least one southern association had a full-time person to help nonprofits merge.

Still others report a need for downsizing in a period of population decline or stagnation. "We have too many nonprofits in this state," one southern director argued. "There is not as much merger activity as we'd like to see." A northeastern director even reported "a healthy fear of smallness. Many of our nonprofits feel that they are not the right size to compete. They either have to grow rapidly and muscle up or die."

Whatever they called it, and however they felt about it, the pressure to reengineer was palpable. A general sense of fear imbued the sample of association directors, a sense that change was inevitable. The key question was not so much whether their nonprofits would have to find new ways of operating, but who would do the initiating. Although a strong resistance was felt to the reengineering ideology as imported from the corporate world, there was surprisingly little capacity to help nonprofits find appropriate partners. Beyond the Maryland Management Innovation Fund and a full-time staff person to support mergers in Tennessee, the other seventeen states were mostly on their own to let the market work its will on the sector with or without the kind of thoughtful analysis suggested by La Piana and others.

The lack of guidance is clearly not a problem with efforts to open the nonprofit sector to a more watchful eye. Most nonprofits are required by law to file the Form 990, and plenty of accounting firms are ready to prepare the documentation for nonprofits with the funding. The question for this tide of reform is not who will provide the help, but whether the sunshine will act as the hoped-for odium or merely create more work for already overstressed nonprofits.

As with the two previous tides, the transparency movement has its advocates and opponents. Some association directors saw the advantages of the movement for provoking needed technological advancements. "Our small- to medium-sized nonprofits will have to get better," said a southern director. "Right now, they don't have the technology to put their 990s up on the Internet, and can't do more than the minimum on filling out the forms. But this pushes them harder and they'll have to make the upgrades. Foundations need to know that they need to make some investments here, otherwise this is going nowhere. Right now, most of the forms are being filled out by hand." A western director agreed: "The vast majority of our nonprofits are still unaware of this information, that it's a requirement. We'll see a real revolution as they go through it. It's a public education effort to inform the nonprofits, even though the goal is ultimately to inform the public. This may raise the bar for technological competence among nonprofits."

A Midwestern director even argued that the transparency effort may increase public confidence, echoing at least some of the rhetoric of national advocates such as GuideStar: "Our best supporter is an informed citizen. All 990s in this state have been on the web for four years. Since nonprofits are like business, and a business's goal is to make money and they can show it, nonprofits should be able to show a measure of what they do."

Not surprisingly given the other tides, other associations see the transparency effort as a waste of precious resources. "This is off the radar screen of most nonprofits," said a western director. "The 990 data is terrible now, so increased visibility will likely improve the quality of the data. But so what? Most nonprofits file their 990s now without a single board member taking a look. It is just background noise, not an accountability mechanism." A Midwestern director agreed, arguing that "the 990s are so abysmally put together that it's only going to be a big story for big nonprofits. The choice is to upgrade computers to do the 990s online or serve ten families. The 990s are only going to be relevant for the organizations that have the money to buy the technology, and that isn't the majority of our members."

As for the larger organizations, one southern director reported that her "groups gasped when she suggested posting the 990s on their websites. It is a little bit shocking to know that someone might look at this stuff. Our groups are very passionate about what they do and get very passionate enemies who they fear will use this information to push stories to the press. They don't want to spend enormous time defining themselves when they have real work to do and are hoping this will all go away."

Moreover, several directors argued that the transparency movement will succeed only if donors learn what the 990s mean. "The 990s are the best tool a donor has right now," said a southern director, "but they don't know how to interpret the information and it's too dense to access. Have you ever tried to make sense of the data on those forms? It is a nightmare." Capacity building for the reform involves more than just technological competence. It also involves teaching consumers, including the press, how to use the new information wisely. If the Form 990 becomes just another tool for digging dirt, the resistance will increase.

Liberation management is currently at its crest in the states, driven in part by the United Way of America's push for outcomes measurement and by the new marketization created by government outsourcing. Before turning to these two parts of the tide, it is important to note the decline of total quality management. As originally championed by W. Edwards Deming, TQM seeks consistency above all else. Only through consistency of effort can manufacturers reduce errors, only through the reduction of errors to zero can they assure maximum market share and customer satisfaction.[99] Having reached its crest in the early to mid-1990s, TQM is in decline. Asked about TQM, one mid-Atlantic director simply remarked, "Ho hum." A southern director agreed: "We talk about TQM as part of the strategic planning services we provide to nonprofits, but aren't sure the nonprofits know what to do with it. They clearly don't like the terms we use, and are mostly doing it in social services because the state tells them to do it."

Total quality management has faded for three basic reasons. First, the language of TQM was so contrary to the core beliefs of most nonprofits that it simply could not be sustained. "Our nonprofits hated the concept," one western director remembered. "They just don't want to see themselves locked into that kind of transaction. There's enough out there already to make them think they are becoming like Burger King. Setting service standards rankled them, insulted them, took away some of their pride. They didn't want to be short-order cooks."

Second, the TQM methodology was so complex that most nonprofits simply could not implement the full reform. Although TQM is easily pilloried as little more than customer service standards, it involves a highly sophisticated statistical process. Business processes such as welfare intake are broken down into their most basic elements and analyzed for potential improvement. Most nonprofits, indeed most businesses, do not have the resources to make the full commitment.

Third, and perhaps most worrisome for full implementation of other nonprofit reforms, TQM required a long-term commitment to change. Any nonprofit that expected TQM to make a difference in a year or two was deluding itself. Most of the reforms described in this report take time.

It remains to be seen, therefore, whether the two active components of liberation management will remake the sector. Outcomes measurement is at high tide. All but one of the nineteen states reported that the reform idea is present, and twelve said it was intense. Of those twelve, two-thirds mentioned the United Way of America effort as one reason for the crest. "Before the United Way campaign," one southern director argued, "most of the focus was on the needs of the client. Now people are really looking to the needs of the funders. The push is now spilling over to non-United Way agencies, kind of infusing the state with this notion that outcomes matter. All in all, it is a good thing for us, but there's also some concern that scarce resources are being used more to jump through the hoops than actually serve clients."

High tide or not, there is still considerable reluctance toward the idea. Some of the frustration involves resources. "There are absolutely no resources for satisfying these United Way requirements, but we sure know that this matters," a Midwestern director noted. "We've had several prominent local groups lose funding because they couldn't specify a clear outcome, and that sent a strong signal that you better learn how to do this." And a western director argued that nonprofits "need to get out of the trap of responding to the latest category or tool that funders establish, while doing something useful for ourselves."

Some of the frustration involves definitions. "Everybody is asking for outcomes-based management," a southern director reported. "The United Ways in this state are really into it. It's tied into every proposal a nonprofit writes now. We don't really know what it means so we're figuring it out based on what's asked and who's doing the asking. The United Ways supply templates to tell local nonprofits how to fill this all out, which is fine. But that can also produce a lot of parroting back. There's a real lack of connection here between what funders want and what nonprofits know."

Finally, some of the frustration is based in a belief that funders have not engaged the nonprofit sector in a dialogue about the value of the effort. One reason the Maryland standards effort has generated so much enthusiasm within the community is that it was developed by nonprofits for nonprofits. Although the United Way of America involved the sector in its conversations and included representatives of the YMCA of America and Girl Scouts on its Task Force on Impact, the effort was heavily weighted toward funders, advocates, and academics, which gave its final recommendations a slight patina of distance.

Notwithstanding these concerns, the outcomes movement is clearly ascendant for the time being. "It is time-consuming but valuable," one Midwestern executive said. "The big issue is that the evaluative methods keep changing, which causes no end to the frustration. Five years ago everyone was into longer-term evaluative methods. Today, it is very much show us what you've accomplished in a year. There is a real focus on showing results as fast as you can, and that drives nonprofits to count things as outcomes that are not appropriate." If outcomes measurement is to stick, some funders apparently need to learn the definitions, too.

The question for many nonprofits is how outcomes measurement might help them compete against the marketization of the sector. And that question is still mostly unanswered. A very large proportion of the association directors sees the marketization as a looming issue. It is present in ten of the states, and active in two. Some states have such strong local controls that a Lockheed Martin IMS is wise to look elsewhere for business, while others have opened the gates to all comers. Reading through the interviews, there is clearly more fear than reality. But the fear is most certainly motivating. "Lockheed is negotiating with the state to take over the welfare system," one southern director noted. "Even if it doesn't affect a particular nonprofit, it's the kind of thing that gets in the papers and makes everyone edgy. It has ramped up interest in training on mergers and financial management."

The marketization has a somewhat different effect in states such as Delaware and Florida where private firms such as Lockheed Martin IMS and Maximus have become paymasters to collections of nonprofits. The rise of for-profit intermediaries has produced a mix of relief at the timeliness of payments and a growing concern about how the profit motive might eventually cut into nonprofit resources. In one Midwestern state, the marketization has even produced a surge in what one director described as the "creaming of the sector as nonprofit people start for-profits to get in on the growth."

When one steps back from these specific comments about marketization, outcomes, or any of the other tides, one gets a sense of the enormous complexity of the sector and the general confusion about what any given nonprofit might do to compete, get better, produce greater outcomes, or raise the bar on performance. Although the interviews suggest that the nonprofit sector feels the funding pressure and the demand to show results, they also confirm the shallowness of the embrace of any given reform idea. Yes, nonprofits will put their Form 990s on the web where possible, and yes, they will fill out the outcome templates that are required for United Way funding. They will also get better at financial statements and job descriptions, if that is what their circle of funders ask.

But one comes away from even a brief reconnaissance musing about the lack of an indigenous commitment to any particular reform. But for occasional exceptions here and there, the sector has yet to declare its interest in a specific reform. It picks ideas that work, jettisons those that do not, but rarely has the time or technical assistance that might fit a particular idea with a mission-based reality.

The Depth of Knowledge

The United States has always been a nation of voluntary associations. "Americans of all ages, all stations in life, and all types of disposition are forever forming associations," wrote Tocqueville in *Democracy in America*. "There are not only commercial and industrial associations in which all take part, but others of a thousand different parts—religious, moral, serious, futile, very general and very limited, immensely large and very minute. . . . Nothing, in my view, deserves more attention than the intellectual and moral associations in America."[100]

Unfortunately, organization theorists have given scant attention to Tocqueville's recommendation. Funding for research on nonprofit organizations has been dwarfed by funding for studies of just about every other organization known to human kind, most of which involve profit making. Although the Aspen Institute's Nonprofit Sector Research Fund continues to provide modest funding for sector-specific research, the general strategy of late has been to cull the private sector for lessons that might translate easily into nonprofit settings. Hence, Christine W. Letts, William P. Ryan, and Allen Grossman start their book *High Performance Nonprofit Organizations* by acknowledging their interest in seeing "whether and how business methods could be adapted, or already have been adapted to support nonprofit goals." As they explain, this cross-sector mapping offers two benefits:

> First, examining nonprofit issues in relief against another sector helps identify how the nonprofit environment influences the decisions and behaviors of managers and practitioners. It can produce what has been called "bisociation"—wherein compelling new insights emerge when dissimilar things are compared. . . . Second, businesses are generally dedicated to growth, which was how we initially conceived of the challenge of increasing social impact. From this angle, it seemed that a cross-sector inquiry could uncover techniques, methods, or perspectives that might be useful to nonprofits that wanted to expand their programs or organizations.[101]

There is nothing at all wrong with such an effort, particularly when it is carefully bounded by a core understanding of what makes the nonprofit sector different, which is how Letts and her colleagues approach their task. However, the fascination with corporate success can breed a hubris about the level of knowledge underpinning those lessons learned, which in turn can create a constant churning of reform as fads such as total quality management rise for a moment or two and quickly fade. Because no one knows for sure that a given reform cannot work, and because not enough research has been done on the links between management and performance, advocates are free to make whatever claims they wish about the efficacy of any given reform.

The result is that the rise of a given idea may have much more to do with who endorses it and how much power they have than any real knowledge that implementation will produce the hoped-for improvements, making it easy for advocates to jump from what I have labeled "preferred states of organizational being" to absolute requirements for organizational success. Other things being equal, scholars would likely agree that all nonprofit organizations should have job descriptions, regular board meetings, training funds, and talented leadership. But that does not mean that any of those factors are either necessary or sufficient for success. Plenty of successful organizations do well without job descriptions and so forth, compensating for weakness in one area by building strength elsewhere.

More to the point of this report, the knowledge base is too thin to make anything beyond tight financial management a requirement. The best one can do is troll the sectors looking for best practices that *might* improve performance.

Innovation provides a nearly perfect example of the gap between what the tides of reform promise and what scholars know. Although innovation may be the most celebrated goal of organizational life, scholars know very little about how to build and sustain an innovating organization—meaning one that innovates frequently. They may know plenty about how to move a single idea from conception to launch, but little about what organizations can do to spark more good ideas to begin with.

The problem is not a lack of research on the topic. Surveying the development of the field from 1989 to 1994, Richard A. Wolfe counted 1,299 journal articles and 351 dissertations on the topic of organizational innovation alone, and another 6,244 journal articles and 1,336 dissertations during the same period on innovation more generally.[102] The expansion has continued into the present. Although the majority of this research deals with private sector innovation, where a single new product can mean a life of profit, standard setters will also find a growing body of research on governmental and public innovation, much of it stimulated by the Ford Foundation's Innovations program.[103]

Nor is the problem a lack of scholarly enthusiasm for innovation. An unmistakable "pro-innovation bias," as Robert Drazin and Claudia Bird Schoonhoven call it, exists across the organizational literature.[104] Innovation is often described as the solution for all that ails organizations, be they private, governmental, or nonprofit. In a financial slump? Invent a new product. Public cynicism on the rise? Launch a new program. Losing donors? Get on the Internet. Even "stick-to-your-knitting" authors such as Tom Peters, of *In Search of Excellence* fame, have joined the innovation bandwagon. Peters now recommends that corporations "Get Innovative or Get Dead," writing that "I've become obsessed with innovation of late. I even dream about it. (Yuk!) Looking back at the turmoil of the eighties, all ten bloody years, set me off."[105]

The reason for no standards for innovation stems from the lack of even the simplest agreement on virtually every key question in the field. As Wolfe argues, "the most *consistent* theme found in the organizational innovation literature is that its research results have been *inconsistent*. The current state of the literature thus offer little guidance to those who want to influence organizational innovation."[106]

To date, the field has yet to adopt a common definition of innovation, let alone reach agreement on what interventions might increase organizational innovativeness. Some define innovation as whatever is new to the organization, while others put the focus on true breakthroughs. As Wolfe concludes, "The underdeveloped state of the innovation literature, in spite of the substantial number of studies and reviews conducted across numerous disciplines suggests that the challenge rests in the complex, context-sensitive nature of the phenomenon itself."[107]

This is not to suggest that the literature holds absolutely no practical counsel whatsoever for struggling innovators. Standard setters might find some insights in the recent scholarship on converting older, noninnovative organizations into product innovators. "Most organizations can produce a successful new product occasionally," write Deborah Dougherty and Cynthia Hardy about old business corporations. "IBM's PC [personal computer] and General Motors' Saturn are good examples. The question is whether they can sustain or repeat what they did" The answer, according to this study of service and product innovations in fifteen large private firms, is to change the organization: "We found that most of these firms were not organized to facilitate innovation: occasionally innovation did occur, but it occurred in spite of the system, not because of it."[108]

Despite the occasional insights, standard setters will come away from the innovation literature dazed. Lacking a common definition of terms and a common basis for inquiry, scholars bask in the extraordinary diversity of the field, leaving standard setters who hope to promote innovation wondering what, if anything, might yield a prescription.

The problem in the literature is not just the lack of agreement on what constitutes innovation (or excellence for that matter), however. It is also in the field's single-minded focus on the individual act of innovation. Simply put, most of the available research is not about designing organizations for innovation, but about bringing single acts of innovation to fruition. The literature is almost devoid of insights on what a nonprofit, or governmental agency, might do to improve the organizational odds that innovation will occur and recur. Scholars have learned a great deal about how public entrepreneurs might grope along to success, use old stuff in new ways, and turn bright ideas into innovation, but relatively less about how those same entrepreneurs might reshape their organizations to support innovation as a more natural act.

This focus on the single success makes perfect sense given the current political climate. As Ford Foundation president Susan Berresford argues, "The Innovations in American Government awards program reminds us that people who work in government can and regularly do create effective solutions to important social programs." For a public convinced that government causes more problems than it solves and that almost anything government does is bound to be wasteful and inefficient, single acts of innovation provide needed proof that public institutions, be they nonprofit or governmental, can succeed from time to time.

Moreover, single acts of innovation may be the best most public agencies can do in a climate of intense hostility and scarce resources. "Yes, innovations exist within the federal government," Gore argued in 1993, "but many work hard to keep their innovations quiet. By its nature, innovation requires a departure from standard operating procedure. In the federal government, such departures invite repercussions. The result is a culture of fear and resignation. To survive, employees keep a low profile. They decide that the safest answer in any given situation is a firm 'maybe.' They follow the rules, pass the buck, and keep their heads down."[109] It is no wonder that scholars would dwell on the single act of innovation when the single act of innovation is so miraculous.

Some of the very best work on managing single acts of innovation comes from business schools. The focus is hardly surprising. After all, what matters most to a successful private firm is not its reputation for innovativeness, but its ability to bring profitable ideas to market. Although overall innovativeness is clearly important to the bottom line, private firms exist in markets in which a single idea such as the Intel's Pentium processor can make the difference between long-term success or failure. For scholars of process theory research, as it is labeled, whether a given idea occurs in a moribund agency or vibrant start-up is immaterial. Both require the same ingredients for success. Although those ingredients may be in greater supply in a vibrant start-up, even the most reluctant organizations can innovate. All they need is an innovative manager, a hero of a sort willing to risk it all for a good idea.

Few scholars have made the argument more effectively than Harold L. Angle and Andrew H. Van de Ven, whose research is designed to give "the innovation manager a road map that indicates how and why the innovation journey unfolds and what paths are likely to lead to success or failure."[110] Like any good road map, Angle and Van de Ven's has a beginning, a middle, and an end, or, as they describe it, "(1) an initiation period, in which events occur that set the stage for launching efforts to develop an innovation; (2) a developmental period, in which concentrated efforts are undertaken to transform the innovative idea into a concrete reality; and (3) an implementation or termination period, in which the innovation is either adopted and institutionalized as an ongoing program, product, or business, or is terminated and abandoned." Wherever the journey takes place, whether in a hostile setting or in relative calm, only by managing each stage of the process well will a single innovation succeed. The focus, therefore, is not on the setting, but the management of the idea.

This focus on single acts of innovation in basically unchangeable settings fits with the third and final trend that might leave standard setters frustrated: most of the literature on nonprofit and governmental innovation focuses on the importance of the individual actor in making innovation occur. Organizations do not innovate, entrepreneurs do.

This is certainly the message from Martin Levin and Mary Bryna Sanger's book *Making Government Work: How Entrepreneurial Executives Turn Bright Ideas into Real Results*, the best book currently available on managing the innovation journey in government. "Success in the public sector depends on skillful executives; management matters," Levin and Sanger write, "and, as this book argues, executives are key to inno-vation."[111] Government will not get more innovative until its "ordinary public managers" get more entrepreneurial. For these innovators-to-be, Levin and Sanger say "just do it," providing simple, accessible advice on how to beat the odds against innovation: capitalize on crisis, scan the environment, make subordinates do what you want them to do, seize a good idea, and build momentum for implementation. This focus on the potential role of individual managers in challenging the prevailing wis-dom is the book's greatest strength.

Unfortunately, it is also the book's single weakness. If innovation is the job of entrepreneurs, the best way to get more innovation is to mold ordi-nary managers into entrepreneurs. If, however, innovation is a character-istic of organizational environments, structure, leadership, and internal systems—that is, for example, if it comes from creating and embracing competition, flattening hierarchies, encouraging employee participation, and establishing learning systems—then the best way to get more inno-vation lies in the more mundane work of organizational reform.

Once again, however, the problem is a nearly complete lack of insight that might provide the basis for any kind of standard-setting exercise. Scholars have long been interested in the link between internal structure and innovativeness. The study of structure and innovation is the oldest theme in the study of private sector innovation. From the beginning of that work, which started with a study of electronics firms in England and Scotland by Tom Burns and G. M. Stalker, innovation has been described as the product of relatively loose organizational structures.

There is no question, therefore, that such a link between what I have called liberation management and innovation could be exploited to increase the frequency of innovation. As Fariborz Damanpour argues, "The challenge for executives is to build congruent organizations both for today's work and tomorrow's innovation. Organizations need to have sufficient internal diversity in strategies, structures, people, and processes to facilitate different kinds of innovation and to enhance organizational learning."[112]

As with so much in the field of organizational design, scholars are some distance from knowing what congruent would be. Even a cursory reading of the literature on the role of internal structure in innovation yields the same kind of contradictions seen in the literature as a whole. Organizations are supposed to be simultaneously loose (decentralized into relatively autonomous units) but tight (strong control from the top), big (extra money for good ideas) but little (everyone has a stake in the organization's success), young (a fresh supply of new people and new ideas) but experienced (stocked with seasoned professionals who know what they are doing), highly specialized (individual employees and units are given narrow pieces of the organization's overall job) but unified (everyone should share the mission).

Some scholars have resolved this tension by arguing for different organizational structure at different stages of the innovation process, a point dating back to Gerald Zaltman, Robert Duncan, and Jonny Holbek's 1973 classic *Innovation and Organizations*, which argued that "the organization must shift its structure as it moves through the various stages of innovation; at the earlier initiation stage a more-organic or less-bureaucratic structure seems most appropriate. Then, as the organization moves to the implementation stage, more-bureaucratic structure becomes appropriate."[113] Scholars of governmental innovation now know better. Switching back and forth from bureaucratic structure to organic is not that easy.

Even where solid evidence describes a clear link between structure and innovation at a specific stage of innovation, it is often so conditional that it cannot be applied. Research suggests, for example, that innovation is more likely when organizations are composed of specialists instead of generalists, employees know who they work for and, therefore, where to go with a good idea, and when organizations are decentralized into many roughly autonomous units instead of centralized around a single leader. At the same time, however, this evidence varies across types of innovation (administrative versus programmatic), scope of innovation (big versus limited), and sector (government, nonprofit, or private).

The warning to reformers from this brief tour of the state of knowledge is unmistakable. Just as scholars know relatively little about creating an innovative nonprofit, they also know relatively little about creating a high-performing nonprofit. Much of the scholarly literature on nonprofit excellence recognizes this reality. Letts and her coauthors make no claims about the one best way to manage upstream to high performance, for example. However well motivated the standards movement might be in trying to raise the bar on quality, it has ample reason to be equally shy about drawing conclusions from what remains a limited knowledge base. As Wolfe concludes in his detailed survey, "There can be no one theory of innovation, as the more we learn, the more we realize that 'the whole' remains beyond our grasp."[114]

CHAPTER FIVE

Conclusion

This reconnaissance suggests that the tides of nonprofit management reform are not only active, but that they also appear to be accelerating. The nonprofit sector and its funders clearly recognize that the environment is changing rapidly. For-profit competition is rising even as the long-expected intergenerational transfer of wealth is under way. New philanthropies are being created almost daily, while the list of America's top ten foundations seems to shift monthly as vast infusions of capital boost well-established foundations such as the David and Lucile Packard Foundation and newly created foundations such as the Bill and Melinda Gates Foundation to new prominence.

The resulting pressure to improve is palpable and well recognized in most nonprofits around the country. Their state and local governments may not be outsourcing, but they are asking harder questions about performance. So, too, are their funders, in part because of the enormous investment in outcomes measurement by the United Way of America. At the same time, the media has become much more aggressive in monitoring the sector. National newspapers such as the *New York Times* and *Washington Post* have established philanthropy beats, and more specialized publications such as the *Chronicle of Philanthropy* have become more active in inspecting the sector. Hence, the *Washington Post*'s regular Federal Page "Philanthropy" column and *Chronicle of Philanthropy*'s new "Caring Donor" page, which reports on the latest ratings by the growing number of watchful eye efforts, and the host of other services now popping up to help donors make the right choice.

Given all the activity, it would be no surprise to find many nonprofits confused about what to do first, let alone what to do at all. Are they to invest in new technology to meet the GuideStar pressure? Or better governance systems? A strategic planning process toward outcomes measurement? Or a strategic alliance of some sort? A state-of-the-art fundraising system? Or a customer service standard? The answer sometimes seems to be yes to all of the above.

Without arguing that nonprofits should hunker down against the winds, this essentially unmediated pressure to get better at all things simultaneously suggests at least three recommendations for the suns, moons, and storm makers in the sector.

First, reformers should stick closer to the knowledge base on what might improve organizational performance. Too much of the contemporary reform debate is driven by the search for business practices that *might* help the nonprofit sector improve. Unfortunately, not enough attention is paid to the question of whether those practices work in the business sector. TQM is only the latest in a long list of business reforms that was eagerly embraced by government and the nonprofit sector before it was fully validated in the private sector.

Second, reformers need to recognize the cost of contradictions across the tides. In this regard, nonprofits are not much different from other organizations. They must set priorities carefully and invest their scarce reform energy on a handful of priorities. Otherwise, they will be torn asunder by the incessant churning that occurs with the rise and fall of reform fads. There may not be a reform standard for picking a reform idea and sticking with it, but that is good common-sense advice to anyone beginning the journey toward ordinary excellence. It is also good advice to national and local funders.

Third, and most important, reformers need to focus more closely on the capacity-building model of accountability. All reform ideas cost something, whether in the monetary cost of new technologies or the human capital costs embedded in relatively thin organizations. Unfortunately, search as one might through the long list of examples provided in this report, few illustrations are available of what I have called capacity-based accountability. Although there are exceptions to the rule, the tides of management reform are driven by compliance accountability in the form of rules and transparency or by performance accountability in the form of a focus on competition and outcomes.

There are numerous intersections between the two, whether in the United Way of America's effort to get its local partners to adopt a common language on outcomes (performance meets compliance) or in the demand that all nonprofits make their missions transparent through variations on the Form 990 (compliance meets performance). But less evidence exists beyond the availability of technical assistance here and there of a general commitment to building the nonprofit sector's ability to implement the new systems and reforms, whether by enhancing its information technology (it will be hard to file returns electronically if the sector does not expand its technological capacity), building new sources of leadership (it will be hard to hold the reform edge if turnover rates continue to rise), and building a working inventory of research-based lessons learned.

Assuming that the nonprofit sector's greatest problem is good people trapped in bad systems, what do the sector and its reform advocates intend to do about fixing the bad systems? Telling a nonprofit that it should make its Form 990 visible on the Internet is one thing, giving it the technology to do so effectively is another; telling a nonprofit to take on the private sector and create new revenue streams is one thing, finding leaders with the experience to do so wisely is another. The standards movement helps identify what is wrong with the systems; the war on waste helps identify the waste and incompetence created as a result; watchful eye makes the problems painfully apparent for all to see; and liberation management instructs the sector on how to discipline its wayward members. But without a commitment to capacity building, reformers merely end up reporting the obvious over and over.

The question is why capacity building is not more prominent in the tides. A first answer is that capacity building is the most expensive, time-consuming path to accountability and arguably the least popular politically. Americans have rightly shown little patience for fraud, waste, and abuse in government programs but have long been unwilling to pay the higher taxes needed for state-of-the-art technology and higher salaries for employees. For funders and external watchdogs, capacity building is also the most difficult to monitor. Unlike compliance, which can be evaluated with a checklist, capacity-based accountability requires much deeper inspection. How does one measure, for example, an organization's core competency in dealing with a changing environment, its creative capacity in addressing new problems, or its perseverance, and even faith, in tackling difficult problems?

A second answer is that compliance accountability produces the very thing that so many reform advocates most crave: information that can be posted, tracked, monitored, packaged, and provided. It is relatively easy to know, for example, whether a given nonprofit has issued a Form 990, but much more expensive to provide the new technology needed to join the Internet. Thus, compliance-based recommendations for improvement tend to be less expensive to implement through the creation of new rules and standards, while performance and capacity-based ideas demand a longer-term investment. Moreover, a new rule can be drafted in a matter of months, while capacity building takes time and money. It is little wonder, therefore, that the nonprofit tides of reform are so heavy on compliance. With scarce resources and the rising use of project grants as the prime funding tool, compliance accountability may be the most that the sector can afford.

The problem is that the tides of reform cannot be harnessed without a sound infrastructure of technical and leadership capacity. The only possible outcome is a deluge of pressure without an ability to respond. The Form 990s may get filed, but the information will be thin or, worse yet, fabricated. The strategic plans will be written, but the strategies and accountability chains will be weak or, worse yet, illusions. The collaborations will be created, but the work will still be divided up by the partners and parceled out to their respective fiefdoms. Compliance almost always produces plenty of evidence of implementation, but lacking a parallel investment in capacity building and a clear sense of how action will produce results, the compliance is almost always false.[115] Absent capacity building, can it be otherwise?

Funders clearly play a special role in building that capacity. Not only could they liberalize the basic rules on indirect costs to include the kinds of system modernization and staff development that might lead to greater effectiveness, but they also have the resources to invest in the research and linking systems that might produce an ordered agenda of reform. They could also guide a long-overdue conversation about what constitutes organizational effectiveness in a rapidly changing environment, while encouraging scholars to work together in the search for lessons learned.

Even as funders strengthen their own learning networks through new organizations such as Grantmakers for Effective Organizations, they must also address the fragmentation of the research, training, and technical assistance networks on which individual nonprofits rely. Such a linking network would be relatively easy to assemble, if only because the number of scholars and practitioners currently engaged in research on the sector is still relatively small, and might start with a structured dialogue about what funders, consultants, advocates, and scholars do and do not know about the costs and benefits of reform.

It would be relatively inexpensive, for example, to sweep back through the vast inventory of case studies, evaluation reports, and research analyses that already exist on nonprofit organizations looking for evidence that different forms of management matter. It would also be relatively easy to identify a set of America's most effective nonprofit organizations, and pivot off that list to explore basic questions of organizational effectiveness and the paths to ordinary excellence. The purpose of such research would not be to develop *the* definitive definition of organizational effectiveness or yet another set of standards for action, but to place management reform in its proper place as one of several competing solutions to the crisis of legitimacy.

With or without that research, the nonprofit sector would do well to take stock of the history of management reform in government and the private sector. The nonprofit sector still has time to avoid the wasted motion that has plagued so many government and private reform efforts. There is no reason to repeat the mistakes or build the needless hierarchy that has left government so unattractive to the nation's most talented public servants or that has doomed so many private firms to global irrelevance and bankruptcy. The first step is simply to recognize that not much is known about what makes organizations more effective, especially if they happen to exist in the nonprofit sector.

Notes

1. Graham T. Allison, "Public and Private Management: Are They Fundamentally Alike in All Unimportant Respects?" paper presented at the Public Management Research Conference, Brookings, Washington, D.C., November 1979.

2. Christine W. Letts, William P. Ryan, and Allen Grossman, *High Performance Nonprofit Organizations: Managing Upstream for Greater Impact* (John Wiley, 1999), p. 4.

3. It is not clear, however, what the recent purchase of Jossey-Bass publishers by John Wiley and Sons will mean for publishing on issues of concern to the nonprofit sector.

4. Melissa M. Stone, Barbara Bigelow, and William Crittenden, "Research on Strategic Management in Nonprofit Organizations: Synthesis, Analysis, and Future Directions," *Administration and Society*, vol. 31, no. 3 (July 1999), pp. 378–423.

5. In Marshall E. Dimock, *Administrative Vitality: The Conflict with Bureaucracy* (Harper and Brothers, 1959), p. 116.

6. Michael Hammer, "Reengineering Work: Don't Automate, Obliterate," *Harvard Business Review* (July/August 1990).

7. This argument comes from Peter Frumkin, who critiqued an earlier version of this report.

8. Paul C. Light, *The Tides of Reform: Making Government Work, 1945–1995* (Yale University Press, 1995), p. 1.

9. For a history of Frederick Taylor's theories of scientific management, see Robert Kanigel, *The One Best Way: Frederick Winslow Taylor and the Enigma of Efficiency* (Viking, 1997).

10. See Michael T. Hannan and John H. Freeman, "The Population Ecology of Organizations," *American Journal of Sociology*, vol. 82, no. 4 (Winter 1977), pp. 929–64.

11. The primer on isomorphism is by Walter W. Powell and Paul J. DiMaggio, *The New Institutionalism in Organizational Analysis* (University of Chicago Press, 1991), see in particular chapter 3.

12. Associated Press, "Donations to Top Charities Rose 16% Last Year," *Washington Post*, November 1, 1999, p. A18.

13. Gabriel Rudney, "The Scope and Dimensions of Nonprofit Activity," in Walter W. Powell, ed., *The Nonprofit Sector: A Research Handbook* (Yale University Press, 1987), p. 58.

14. The 10.2 million figure comes from an overview of *The Nonprofit Almanac 1996–1997: Dimensions of the Independent Sector* (San Francisco: Jossey-Bass, 1997) provided by Independent Sector (www.independentsector.org/programs/research/update_nonprofit.html [April 6, 1998]).

15. Sara Meléndez, "State of the Sector," October 25, 1999 (www.independentsector.org/about/state_of_the_sector.html [December 12, 1999]), p. 3.

16. Samantha Stainbum, "Back to School," *Who Cares* (March/April 1998) (www.whocares.org/marapr98/cover.htm [July 19, 1999]).

17. Lester M. Salamon, *Holding the Center: America's Nonprofit Sector at a Crossroads* (New York: Nathan Cummings Foundation, 1997), pp. xiii–xviii.

18. Independent Sector, "Giving and Volunteering in the United States 1999," fact sheet, October 20, 1999.

19. The University of California, Los Angeles, Higher Education Research Institute found that a record 74 percent of students entering college in the fall of 1998 had given time for volunteering during their last year of high school. Moreover, 42 percent of college freshmen said they had volunteered at least an hour a week, compared with 27 percent in 1987. The survey also found that the vast majority had volunteered of their own volition. Only 21 percent of the freshmen had attended high schools that required community service for graduation. The bad news is that only 19 percent of the students said they expected to continue their community service in college. See the press release for the study at www.gseis.ucla.edu/heri/press98.html [December 29, 1999].

20. Paul C. Light, *The New Public Service* (Brookings, 1999), p. 64.

21. William P. Ryan, "The New Landscape for Nonprofits," *Harvard Business Review* (January/February 1999), p. 128.

22. The Brookings Institution's Center for Public Service, in collaboration with Bryna Mary Sanger of the New School University in New York City, has begun a study of how private firms enter public and nonprofit markets. That reconnaissance will be published in mid-2000, followed by a more detailed census in 2001.

23. Burton A. Weisbrod, "Guest Editor's Introduction: The Nonprofit Mission and Its Financing," *Journal of Policy Analysis and Management*, vol. 17, no. 2 (Spring 1998), p. 167.

24. Ryan, "The New Landscape for Nonprofits," p. 136.

25. Peter Frumkin and Alice Andre-Clark, "When Missions, Markets, and Politics Collide: Values and Strategy in the Nonprofit Human Services," *Nonprofit and Voluntary Sector Quarterly* (forthcoming), p. 1.

26. See, for example, U.S. Merit Systems Protection Board, *The Changing Federal Workplace: Employee Perspectives* (Government Printing Office, 1998).

The Vice President Al Gore "reinventing" package drew heavily upon ideas in good currency during Richard M. Nixon's presidency.

27. The full report can be found in Light, *The New Public Service*.

28. Alceste T. Pappas, *Reengineering Your Nonprofit Organization: A Guide to Strategic Transformation* (John Wiley, 1996), p. 13.

29. See David C. King and Zachary Karabell, "An American Anomaly: The Evolution of Public Trust in the Military from Tet to Tailhook," paper prepared for the Visions of Governance for the 21st Century Project, Harvard University, John F. Kennedy School of Government, November 21, 1998. The Independent Sector started a public education campaign in 1998, but without the kind of funding that would give it the visibility of the armed service recruitment campaigns.

30. See Paul C. Light, *The True Size of Government* (Brookings, 1999).

31. J. Gregory Dees, "Enterprising Nonprofits," *Harvard Business Review* (January/February 1998), p. 13.

32. Frumkin and Clark, "When Missions, Markets, and Politics Collide," p. 4.

33. Peter Frumkin and Mark T. Kim, "Strategic Positions and the Financing of Nonprofit Organizations: Is Efficiency Rewarded in the Contributions Marketplace?" Harvard University, 1998, pp. 8–9.

34. See Christine W. Letts, William Ryan, and Allen Grossman, "Virtuous Capital: What Foundations Can Learn from Venture Capitalists," *Harvard Business Review* (March/April 1997), pp. 2–7.

35. See, for example, Joanne Scheff and Philip Kotler, "How the Arts Can Prosper through Strategic Collaborations," *Harvard Business Review* (January/February 1996); and Alan R. Andreasen, "Profits for Nonprofits: Find a Corporate Partner," *Harvard Business Review* (November/December 1996).

36. Peter Dobkin Hall, "Law, Politics, and Charities in the Post-Liberal Era," unpublished paper, May 1999, p. 1, author's files.

37. United Way of America, *Measuring Program Outcomes: A Practical Approach* (Alexandria, Va., 1996).

38. This mission statement can be found at helping.org (www.helping.org/nonprofit/about.adp [November 1, 1999]).

39. Thomas E. Backer, *Innovation in Context: New Foundation Approaches to Evaluation, Collaboration, and Best Practices,* study conducted for the John S. and James L. Knight Foundation, November 1999, p. 3, author's files.

40. The study, *Keeping the Keepers: Strategies for Association Retention in Times of Attrition*, was conducted by the National Association for Law Placement Foundation (www.nalp.org/Trends/keepers.htm [May 19, 1999]).

41. Weisbrod, "Guest Editor's Introduction," p. 171.

42. Stone, Bigelow, and Crittenden, "Research on Strategic Management in Nonprofit Organizations," p. 408.

43. Robert D. Herman and David O. Renz, "Theses on Nonprofit Organizational Effectiveness," *Nonprofit and Voluntary Sector Quarterly*, vol. 28, no. 2 (June 1999), p. 111.

44. The statement can be found at the Grantmakers for Effective Organizations website (www.geofunders.org/index.htm [October 22, 1998]).

45. Ryan, "The New Landscape for Nonprofits," p. 129.

46. See Stephen Rathgeb Smith and Michael Lipsky, *Nonprofits for Hire: The Welfare State in the Age of Contracting* (Harvard University Press, 1993), for a prescient assessment of the future that is now coming to pass.

47. See Susan Doran, *Saddling Up: Exploring the Need for a D.C. Rider*, a report to the Eugene and Agnes Meyer Foundation, October 9, 1998 (www.techproject.org/meyerreport.html [October 24, 1999]).

48. See Peter Frumkin, "The Long Recoil from Regulation: Private Philanthropic Foundations and the Tax Reform Act of 1969," *American Review of Public Administration*, vol. 28, no. 3 (September 1998).

49. Daniel P. Forbes, "Measuring the Unmeasurable: Empirical Studies of Nonprofit Organization Effectiveness," *Nonprofit and Voluntary Sector Quarterly*, vol. 27, no. 2 (June 1998), pp. 183–202; and Herman and Renz, "Theses on Nonprofit Organizational Effectiveness," p. 121.

50. See Paul C. Light, *Monitoring Government: Federal Inspectors General and the Search for Accountability* (Brookings, 1993), chapter 1.

51. Ibid., p. 15.

52. Al Gore, *From Red-Tape to Results* (Government Printing Office, 1993), p. 3.

53. See Paul C. Light, *Sustaining Innovation: Creating Government and Nonprofit Organizations That Innovate Naturally* (San Francisco: Jossey-Bass, 1998).

54. These standards can be found at www.philanthropy.com/premium/articles/v11/i09/09004202.htm [July 29, 1999].

55. The fund-raising benchmarks can be found at www.fcny.org/mgmt/managing_future.htm [October 24, 1999].

56. The standards are contained in the organization's easily accessible booklet "Standards for Excellence: An Ethics and Accountability Code for the Nonprofit Sector" (Baltimore: Maryland Association of Nonprofit Organizations, 1998), p. 26; my appreciation to Peter Berns and Mara L. Winters for sharing this material.

57. Anthony Giorgianni, "Ohio United Way Requires Charities to Pass Review by Outside Group," *Chronicle of Philanthropy*, February 25, 1999 (www. philanthropy.com/premium/articles/v11/i09/09004201.htm [July 29, 1999]).

58. Lester Salamon was on the advisory board that developed the standards.

59. Standards for Excellence Application Package and Checklist, author's files.

60. Herman and Renz, "Theses on Nonprofit Organizational Effectiveness," pp. 115, 116.

61. Many of the assessment systems now percolating through the sector use four- or five-point scales to assess organizational adequacy.

62. Gore, *From Red-Tape to Results*, pp. 31–32.

63. Scheff and Kotler, "How the Arts Can Prosper," p. 4.

64. Ibid., p. 11.

65. David La Piana, *Beyond Collaboration: Strategic Restructuring of Nonprofit Organizations* (San Francisco and Washington, D.C.: James Irvine Foundation and National Center for Nonprofit Boards, revised edition, 1997).

66. Hammer, "Reengineering Work."

67. La Piana, *Beyond Collaboration*, p. 3.

68. For a description of the Management Innovation Fund (MI Fund), visit the Maryland Association of Nonprofit Organizations website at www.mdnonprofit.org/mias.htm.

69. Thomas H. Davenport, "The Fad That Forgot People," *Fast Company* (1995) (www.fastcompany.com/onling /01/reengin.html [June 28, 1999]).

70. Letts, Ryan, and Grossman, "Virtuous Capital."

71. Elizabeth Hubbard, "Making Sense of Public Service Partnerships: Understanding the Why and How of Interagency Efforts," unpublished paper, 1995, p. 3, author's files.

72. The following discussion is drawn heavily from Light, *Sustaining Innovation.*

73. The full history of the statute and citations to this portion of the act can be found in Light, *Tides of Reform*, pp. 32–37.

74. Regina E. Herzlinger, "Can Public Trust in Nonprofits and Governments Be Restored?" *Harvard Business Review* (March/April 1996), p. 101.

75. These are preliminary findings from a project funded by the Pew Charitable Trusts. The five agencies studied were the Social Security Administration, the Internal Revenue Service, the Federal Aviation Administration, the Food and Drug Administration, and the Environmental Protection Agency. This contact-to-trust relationship was found among the different customer sets interviewed, including individual and corporate taxpayers as well as tax preparers and individual Social Security recipients, taxpayers, and pension officers.

76. See the Pew Research Center for the People and the Press, *Deconstructing Distrust: How Americans View Government* (Washington, D.C.: Pew Research Center, 1998), for the data.

77. This mission statement can be found at www.nccs.urban.org/about_nccs.html [August 17, 1999], p. 4.

78. The bill of rights can be found at www.guidestar.org/phil/easy0004.html.

79. The outline can be found at www.independentsector.org/giving_voice/initiative.html [August 12, 1999].

80. The outline can be found at www.mncn.org/990pack.htm [August 15, 1999].

81. See *Chronicle of Philanthropy*, October 23, 1999.

82. Gore, *From Red-Tape to Results*, p. 4.

83. David Osborne and Ted Gaebler, *Reinventing Government: How the Entrepreneurial Spirit Is Transforming the Public Sector* (New York: Plume, 1993); and Tom Peters and Richard Waterman, *In Search of Excellence* (HarperCollins, 1982).

84. Lynton Caldwell, *The Administrative Theories of Hamilton and Jefferson* (Columbia University Press, 1938), p. 136.

85. Office of Management and Budget, *Preparation and Submission of Budget Estimates,* OMB Circular No. A-11, Part 2 (Government Printing Office, July 1998), pp. 1–2.

86. Ibid., pp. 1–2.

87. United Way of America, "Report Pending on Current United Way Activities in Measuring Program Outcomes and Community Change," *Measuring*

Impact of United Way (August 1995) (www.unitedway.org/outcomes/impnw11.htm [October 20, 1999]), p. 3.

88. Margaret C. Plantz, Martha Taylor Greenway, and Michael Hendricks, "Outcome Measurement: Showing Results in the Nonprofit Sector," *Online Resource Library* (July 1999) (www.unitedway.org/outcomes/ndpaper.htm [October 20, 1999]), p. 15.

89. *Weekly Compilation of Presidential Documents* (Government Printing Office, October 17, 1994).

90. For an exception, see Demetra Smith Nightingale and Nancy Pindus, "Privatization of Public Social Services: A Background Paper," paper prepared at the Urban Institute, Washington, D.C., October 15, 1997 (www.urban.org/pubman/privatiz.htm [August 30, 1999]); see also the information provided at www.welfareinfo.org.

91. These examples are drawn from the WIN website (www.welfareinfo.org/privitization.htm [October 28, 1999]); no updates are provided on the site from 1999, which may indicate that the project has moved its staff resources to other areas.

92. Edward Skloot, "Education, Privatization, and the Future of Human Services," speech delivered at the Annual Conference of the Council on Foundations, New Orleans, La., April 21, 1999.

93. Laurie Paarlberg and Kristen Gronbjerg, *Nonprofit Fee-for-Service Income*, report prepared for the Aspen Institute's Nonprofit Strategy Group (July 26, 1999), p. 9, author's files.

94. Mark Rosenman, with Kristen Scotchmer, *Morphing into the Market: The Danger of Missing Mission,* report prepared for the Aspen Institute's Nonprofit Strategy Group (1999), p. 12.

95. "Raiders of the Lost Jobs," *Public Employee* (January/February 1998), p. 64.

96. The program brochure is in the author's files.

97. Thomas K. Reis and Stephanie J. Clohesy, "Unleashing New Resources and Entrepreneurship for the Common Good: A Scan, Synthesis, and Scenario for Action," paper released by the W. K. Kellogg Foundation, January 1999, p. 6.

98. The telephone survey of association executive directors was conducted in August and September 1999. In all, forty state associations were asked for an interview. Despite repeated call-backs, some of the directors never responded, while others were impossible to schedule.

99. See W. Edwards Deming, *Out of the Crisis* (Massachusetts Institute of Technology, 1982).

100. Alexis de Tocqueville, *Democracy in America*, ed. J. P. Mayer, tran. George Lawrence (Garden City, N.Y.: Harper Perennial, 1988), pp. 513, 517.

101. Letts, Ryan, and Grossman, *High Performance Nonprofit Organizations*, pp. 4–5.

102. Richard A. Wolfe, "Organizational Innovation: Review, Critique, and Suggested Research Directions," *Journal of Management Studies,* vol. 31, no. 3 (1994), pp. 425–26.

103. Alan A. Altshuler and Mark Zegans, "Innovation and Creativity: Comparisons between Public Management and Private Enterprise," *CITIES* (February 1990), pp. 16–24.

104. Robert Drazin and Claudia Bird Schoonhoven, "Community, Population, and Organization Effects on Innovation: A Multilevel Perspective," *Academy of Management Journal*, vol. 39, no. 5 (1996), pp. 1065–83.

105. Tom Peters, "Get Innovative or Get Dead," *California Management Review*, vol. 33, no. 4 (1990), p. 9.

106. Wolfe, "Organizational Innovation," p. 426.

107. Ibid., pp. 405–06.

108. Deborah Dougherty and Cynthia Hardy, "Sustained Product Innovation in Large, Mature Organizations: Overcoming Innovation-to-Organization Problems," *Academy of Management Journal*, vol. 39, no. 5 (1996), p. 1121.

109. Gore, *From Red-Tape to Results*, pp. 2–3.

110. Harold L. Angle and Andrew H. Van de Ven, "Suggestions for Managing the Innovation Journey," in Andew H. Van de Ven, Harold L. Angle, and M. S. Poole, eds., *Research on the Management of Innovation: The Minnesota Studies* (Harper and Row, 1989), p. 663.

111. Martin Levin and Mary Bryna Sanger, *Making Government Work: How Entrepreneurs Turn Bright Ideas into Real Results* (San Francisco: Jossey-Bass, 1994), p. ii.

112. Fariborz Damanpour, "Organizational Innovation: A Meta-Analysis of Effects of Determinants and Moderators," *Academy of Management Journal*, vol. 34, no. 3 (1991), p. 92.

113. Gerald Zaltman, Robert Duncan, and Jonny Holbeck, *Innovation and Organizations* (Wiley, 1973), p. 115.

114. Wolfe, "Organizational Innovation," p. 12.

115. The John S. and James L. Knight Foundation has begun a survey of innovation nonprofit capacity-building programs funded or operated by North American foundations. The survey, to be conducted by Human Interaction Research Institute under the direction of Tom Backer, should be completed in 2000.

Index